Canadian Biography Series

PETER GZOWSKI: AN ELECTRIC LIFE

Peter Gzowski in 1982.
PHOTO COURTESY THE CBC

Peter Gzowski

AN ELECTRIC LIFE

Marco Adria

ECW PRESS

CANADIAN CATALOGUING IN PUBLICATION DATA

Adria, Marco, 1959–
Peter Gzowski : an electric life
Includes bibliographical references.
ISBN 1-55022-166-3

1. Gzowski, Peter. 2. Radio broadcasters –
Canada – Biography. I. Title.

PN1991.4.G97A42 1994   791.44'092   C94-932050-1

This book has been published with the assistance of the Ministry
of Culture, Tourism and Recreation of the Province of Ontario,
through funds provided by the Ontario Publishing Centre, and with
the assistance of grants from the Department of Canadian Heritage,
The Canada Council, the Ontario Arts Council, and the Government
of Canada through the Canadian Studies and Special Projects
Directorate of the Department of the Secretary of State of Canada.

Design and imaging by ECW Type & Art, Oakville, Ontario.
Printed by Imprimerie Gagné, Louiseville, Québec.

Distributed by General Distribution Services,
30 Lesmill Road, Toronto, Ontario M3B 2T6.
(416) 445-3333, (800) 387-0172 (Canada), FAX (416) 445-5967.

Published by ECW PRESS,
2120 Queen Street East, Suite 200,
Toronto, Ontario M4E 1E2.

ACKNOWLEDGEMENTS

I thank Bob Bossin, Ted Byfield, and Mel Hurtig for their insights into Peter Gzowski's role in Canadian media; Edna Barker for comments and suggestions on two drafts of the book; Kerry Cannon for helping with the research; Peter Gzowski himself for talking to me, first in 1987 as his fifth season on *Morningside* was coming to a close, then in 1992 at the end of the tenth, when we talked about his childhood and adolescence; B.W. Powe for discussing with me the relationship between the written word and the broadcast word in Canada; and Bill Ramp for his observations on mass media in Canada, which I used in Chapter 4.

TABLE OF CONTENTS

LIST OF ILLUSTRATIONS

PREFACE

What are electricity and radio if not action at a distance?
— Casaubon, in *Foucault's Pendulum*, by Umberto Eco

Two themes converge in this account. That meeting makes, I think, a consideration of the events of Peter Gzowski's life and career especially timely. The themes are Canadian nationalism on the one hand and, on the other, the tension between the written word and the broadcast word. I am not the first to consider these themes at once: B. W. Powe, in *The Solitary Outlaw*, which appeared in 1987, has examined the lives and work of other distinguished Canadians in the context of the decline of the written word. He has retrieved the notion of the printed word as a technology for setting off public explosions of rhetoric or polemic in a milieu in which electrical connections have all but swamped dialogue.

Peter Gzowski provides a prickly case study for an examination of the relationship between Canadian nationalism and the emerging tension between the written and the broadcast word. This case is encapsulated for me in two statements Gzowski has made. The first is from a conversation he had in 1986 with the journalist Mark Abley; the second is a comment he made to me a year or so later:

This country is my beat.
I'm a writer who's now working in radio.

In these pages, some of the implications of these two statements are considered. In Chapter 2, for example, I suggest that Gzowski's conception of Canada's regions — and the passion for national unity he lays over this conception — seems to have been influenced by his brief residence, early in his career, in two small Canadian cities, Timmins and Moose Jaw. And the job of "newspaperman" (as he would have called it then) provided the beginnings of a career in which his sense of nationalism, a product of both his family and community upbringing, could be nurtured and expressed.

★

The main incidents in Gzowski's life and career must be considered in a cultural context of awakening and growth in Canada. The most recent rise of Canadian nationalism — the beginnings of which we may mark with the centenary celebrations of 1967 — has seen the development of both a market for Canadian culture and an infrastructure for the production of the artefacts of that culture. Canadian literature in the early 1960s, for example, was a narrow field with few proponents. The most singular of these advocates was professor and critic Malcolm Ross, who, in 1958, began the New Canadian Library, published by McClelland and Stewart. Today Canadian literature is thriving, with hundreds of new titles released every year and with a gangly body of criticism growing around it. But concurrent with the dynamic expansion of a traditional cultural activity such as writing — and this is where Gzowski comes in — was an expansion of the new cultural "industries" in Canada, of which broadcast and recording represented the most dramatic growth.

Although there were few obstacles to his rise to national prominence, Gzowski grew up with an ambivalent sense of citizenship. As a child, he found psychic refuge in listening to *American* radio but he remained conscious of his family forebears' role in asserting Canada's sovereignty in North America. In his young adulthood, he covered this ambivalence with ambition. He moved quickly through a succession of jobs as a journalist, finding particular success in 1971 as the innovative host of a CBC Radio program called *This Country in the Morning*, a fortuitous discovery that has shaded his career since that time. The rapid climb to success was made possible by a robust Canadian economy and by a rapidly expanding CBC, which is itself the heaviest of Canada's cultural instruments.

Also in these pages, I discuss what kind of "noise" *Morningside* makes and why it does so. Literally, of course, the show as noise provides an aural background for many Canadians' — especially women's — daily activities. Figuratively, the noise of *Morningside* constitutes a social signal that has yet to be discerned by social critics. Gzowski's personal role in the signals emanating from the show and from the CBC is significant.

Referring to this phenomenon, the narrator of a National Film Board feature says,

> For three hours every morning, he turns the country into a neighbourhood, letting us know how other Canadians are making it through their day. (*Family*)

By examining the themes of his family heritage and worldview, I will suggest that "*Morningside* as neighbourhood" is an appropriate description of the view Gzowski has of his work on radio and that this view is connected directly to the noise the CBC makes.

★

In company with all the other *Morningside* listeners I have met, I am a dedicated fan of Peter Gzowski's. He is simply the best broadcaster working in Canada. If such a thing as a national life exists, Canada's life is enriched by honouring someone whose acclaim is based on his acumen in asking questions, whose daily task is to open up and carry on a conversation, rather than to try to close a debate, which is often the function of political life in Canada. If some passages in this study seem critical of Gzowski's stance and position in Canadian media, it is partly because he is one of the handful of media figures who through their work have insisted on a significant place in public life and discourse. I dedicate the book to Prof. T.H.B. Symons, whose life and work — like Gzowski's — provide evidence that Canada may yet be inhabited by Canadians.

M.A.

February 18, 1994

Peter Gzowski

AN ELECTRIC LIFE

1. Galt

THREE LIVES

Peter Gzowski puts his feet up and tips his chair back against the window of his cramped office in CBC Radio's Jarvis Street headquarters in Toronto. Gzowski likes to put his feet up. And he likes cigarettes. That's why a grey-blue haze of smoke surrounds him, making it difficult to know whether he's looking at me or out the door into the chaos of furniture, magazines, and typewriters that is the base of operations for his radio program called *Morningside*. He is talking about laziness and about nicotine addiction. He says he suffers from both. His laziness, he claims, is the reason he works so hard, and his nicotine addiction, he points out, is one of the things his listeners like about him. Well, here is a public figure who catalogues his weaknesses, discusses them with as many people as will listen, and makes a career of the thing. I love it, and so do the approximately one million Canadians who tune in to *Morningside* daily.

Gzowski appeals to me (and, I presume, to the other members of his audience) on three levels, which may be considered his "lives." First is the *social* life. Through his role as a broadcaster, Gzowski has made a deliberate attempt to contribute to the cause of Canadian unity and to notions of the Canadian identity.

This attempt is entwined, in turn, with the CBC's role in promoting unity. But Gzowski has brought a personal commitment to the effort. That commitment was borne from his particular view of Canadian life, which can be traced to the experience of growing up in a small southern Ontario town. The second life is connected to the *professional* milieu in which Gzowski has worked, the mass media. Beginning as a writer, then transferring his skills to the electronic media, Gzowski has been concerned throughout his career with questioning and defining the role of the journalist. His influence on other journalists has been most evident in the persona and sensibility he brought to *Morningside* when he became host of the program in 1981.

Finally — and this brings me back to the portrait of Gzowski in the veils of his cigarette smoke — there is the *personal* life, which is typified for his audience, of course, by the distinctive deep voice, the famous stammer, the cigarettes, and the hints given by Gzowski himself of overindulgence. More broadly considered, it is the life in which the other biographical strands may be seen to converge. It has its beginnings, and its most meaningful resonances, in the small town. It is the level at which the audience tunes in daily. And it is our point of departure for an examination of Gzowski's life.

These three lives can be considered in another way. Gzowski has lived, like many other Canadians, a social, professional (or vocational), and personal life. He has also drawn his conception of human relations according to a personal mythology — a "story" devised to help make sense of the many influences that have affected his world-view. For Gzowski, *family* was an important set of human relations from an early age, a fact made clear by the preservation in memory, anecdote, and document of the accomplishments of Sir Casimir Gzowski, Peter's paternal great-great-grandfather. However, his actual relations within the family were cut short, first by the divorce of his parents — which severed a living connection with the heritage of Sir Casimir, since Peter would live apart from his father almost from infancy — then by the death of his mother when Peter was still a teenager.

FIGURE I

Sir Casimir Gzowski.
PHOTO COURTESY THE ONTARIO ARCHIVES, S 17159

FIGURE 2

Sir Casimir Gzowski's residence, "The Hall."
PHOTO COURTESY THE ONTARIO ARCHIVES, ACC. 2309 S 2903

Perhaps as a result of this sudden and early alienation from family, Gzowski placed great emphasis in childhood on the relations of *community*; at least this is what seems clear from his recollections of that period. Gzowski looks back with fondness to his boyhood in Galt. There, dignity and decency, he recalls, were instilled in a climate in which the roles of the businessman, publisher, politician, and family member were distinct yet connected. While a resident of Galt was expected to fulfil a particular role to contribute to the welfare of the community, that role's complementarity with other roles was maintained by a common set of values, which I will discuss further when I examine Gzowski's Galt.

The *nation* is the third and largest set of human relations that can be considered with regard to Gzowski's life. With this set of relations — and this is one of the fascinating and appealing features of Gzowski's *Morningside* — he would synthesize his conceptions of family, community, and nation in the presentation of his radio persona. His own family broken (his daughter Alison said he never learned to be a father), Gzowski became fatherly in oration and visage: listening carefully, speaking only occasionally with that wonderful voice, growing a grey beard. Setting in motion a transcontinental surge of empathy and understanding, *Morningside* revealed a father for the nation, a substitute for all the paternal love untendered. When some were asking, "Who will speak for Canada?" Gzowski answered, "Good morning . . . I'm Peter Gzowski . . . This is *Morningside*."

We should note at the outset that for each revelation Gzowski has made concerning his personal life, there is a corresponding silence. While he has discussed the anguish of losing his mother when he was still an adolescent, for example, he will not discuss the reasons for the domestic unhappiness that contributed to that anguish. When asked why he was unhappy as a child, he says that he doesn't talk about this much, that he hopes to sort out his feelings on the matter in a book he wants to write about his mother and father. I asked him the question in the busy ambience of his office at CBC Radio. As he answered, sirens began

FIGURE 3

Sir Casimir and his family, c. 1860.

PHOTO COURTESY THE ONTARIO ARCHIVES, S 4308

to sound from Jarvis Street, a couple of floors below; an ambulance was in service. Because his window was open to allow cigarette smoke to escape from the "non-smoking" offices of the cbc, the wailing was impossible to ignore. He turned to my tape-recorder microphone and said, "For the record, sirens always go off when I talk about this subject" ("Interview," 1992 [Adria]).

The stance is taken regularly. Gzowski offers frank observations or recollections, which, while appearing to be windows onto his feelings, turn out to be doors. They are a means of protecting a core of pain, not a means of revelation. Similarly, when he talks or writes about his children, as he does often, the listener or reader may be justified in believing that Gzowski considers his relationships to be a delicate but significant means of defining his public persona. But he has revealed all he cares to concerning those relationships; the few sensitive and personal details he has discussed in his books and columns, in media interviews, and on radio have been chosen and elaborated on carefully, requiring in Gzowski's mind, it seems, no further discussion.

This point needs to be mentioned now because for our consideration of Gzowski's "personal" life, there is much that for the time being must remain unsaid. Ironically, this absence of personal revelation at the centre of Gzowski's public persona apparently evokes a measure of empathy. He finds friendly company with all those members of his audience who have tried to define their present personal circumstances in relation to their past experiences, while keeping their backward gaze carefully averted from those events that are too painful or delicate to mention. Adopting the sensibility of the resident of a small town, Gzowski manifests the belief that personal and social cohesion may be strengthened — albeit perhaps temporarily — by keeping some matters to himself.

We must therefore weave a depiction of Gzowski's personal life after sorting the strands of what we know of his professional and social lives. An understanding of the outlines of his divorce, for example, or what seem to be complicated relations with his children, may be divined only after we understand the professional and social assumptions that have informed the important decisions of his personal life. Many of his publicly offered reflections have their source in Galt. In Galt, Gzowski experienced a wounded family life, learned the custom and convention of life in a small town, and acquired a respect for the habits of ambition and enterprise. These gleanings were to strain the familial bonds throughout his later life. They are thus a set of first principles for a consideration of Peter Gzowski's life.

THE SMALL TOWN VIEW

Peter John Gzowski was born to Harold and Margaret Gzowski on July 13, 1934, a Friday, in Toronto. An only child (as was his father), Peter was a welcome intrusion into his parents' lives. However, his parents' marriage quickly lost its footings. Harold's father, Peter's grandfather, Lieutenant Colonel Harold Gzowski, expressed his willingness to help the broken family, and Margaret honoured the gesture. She went to live with "the Colonel," as family members were to refer to him, taking young Peter with her. That Margaret felt able to accept this arrangement, based on the kindness of an estranged husband's father, suggests something of the subtleties of human relations in the Gzowski family, especially as they have been affected by the paternal line. Pride and charity have enjoyed a conspicuous currency in the family, and we shall see that Peter himself has not devalued them in his personal dealings.

The first few years of Peter's life were spent in Toronto, where both parents had roots, and these years were otherwise uneventful. A snapshot from those times, taken on a balmy day in 1938, shows Peter on a garden swing, apparently contented and relaxed in the summer sun (figure 4).

Peter's mother tried to find a sense of personal achievement

FIGURE 4

Peter in June 1938.
PHOTO COURTESY OF PETER GZOWSKI

FIGURE 5

Peter (four years old) and Margaret, his mother, in 1939.
PHOTO COURTESY OF PETER GZOWSKI

by variously attending library school and working at the book department at Eaton's. When Peter was four his mother remarried and the family moved to Galt, where his new stepfather, Reginald Brown, worked for a textile manufacturer. Peter took his stepfather's surname. A photo from 1939 shows a somewhat serious-looking Peter, dressed in suit jacket, tie, and short pants, standing with his mother in front of their home (figure 5).

The daughter of a prominent lawyer, Peter's mother had been reared in more auspicious surroundings than those to be found in Galt. She became unhappy in her second marriage. Although Peter's stepfather was dependable — in a way that his natural father was not — and a "nice guy" (*This Country* 14), a measure of gloom was invited by Margaret's dissatisfaction with life in Galt and at home. This created tension in the home, and Peter's unhappiness grew in turn.

Some fifty years later, he would point out to a visitor, as testimony to his mother's unhappiness at that earlier time, a photo in the Galt *Daily Reporter*. There, his mother poses with fellow members of the Galt Badminton Club of 1948–49. The dutiful and dreary report in the town's paper of the activities of a club such as this was typical of the nucleus of a life in Galt and in countless small communities in Canada. Margaret had earned a master's degree from the venerable St. Andrew's University in Scotland. She was young, bright, and outgoing. Now the milestones of her life had become puny events such as the one depicted in the photo. She had expected more. Gazing at the photo, Gzowski would say wryly, "This would *not* have been a great evening in her life" ("Interview," 1992 [Adria]).

He has often spoken and written of his great affection for his mother. On the dedication page of *The Private Voice* appears a poignant photograph of the young Peter (he looks five years old) saluting his mother. He is dressed in what looks like a military outfit or a miniature Mounties uniform. In an interview with Mark Abley for a magazine article in 1986, he said he wished he could have discussed with his mother, later in his life, his aspirations, failures, longings:

One thing has often bothered me deeply since I began to achieve some success. I never got to tell her about it. . . . I'd so like to have lunch with her now. (Abley 23)

The city in which Peter spent his childhood and adolescence does not appear on current maps of southern Ontario. What used to be the city of Galt now forms — along with the former towns of Hespeler and Preston — part of the city of Cambridge, which claims a population of some ninety thousand, and which constitutes part of the municipality of Waterloo. "Old Galt" is now promoted as a tourist attraction by the city of Cambridge. Although the region was consolidated in 1973, there are still some businesses, such as the Galt Shoe Repair, which by their signage refuse to recognize the new arrangement. Heritage is at the foreground of such a city. Galt was founded in 1827 by William Dickson, who was to become a member of the Legislative Council of Upper Canada. The park where Gzowski used to skate as a boy is named after the city's founder. The Grand River runs through the centre of the old city, whose anchor is the historical knitting mill buildings. Like so many other cities in the region, Galt has a Parkhill Road, a Front Street, and a Water Street.

Is there such a thing as a "typical southern Ontario city"? Perhaps not. Each city or town in Canada has a history that renders such generalizations too imprecise to be meaningful. However, for those from another region of Canada who visit a city such as Cambridge for the first time, the experience can be striking. The evidence of a common culture and heritage that existed several decades ago in these cities, and which still exists in some measure, is plain, if only in the architecture that has been saved. The buildings are homely, practical, unpretentious. They were built to last, and they have. Their designers and builders were fashioning a colony, not an outpost. Together, the buildings, streets, and trees of such a city form a tangible core of community.

In southern Ontario, history is the guiding hand of community life. Here, time is accorded a special role in civic life. The

FIGURE 6

24 Park Avenue, Galt (now Cambridge, Ontario), where Peter grew up.
PHOTO COURTESY OF SIMON BURKE AND MAGRELYS RODRIGUES

region's parks, buildings, and civic and cultural institutions are considered important not only for their current status in the lives of residents, but for their status in history, as well. As a result, streets are called by the names of those who settled and civilized southern Ontario. (Might the "civil and peaceable" southern Ontarian — as portrayed by its writers, such as Robertson Davies and Alice Munro — have his or her soul rooted in the injunctions of history?)

In the west, by contrast, places and spaces are the marrow of community life. Gzowski referred to this social fact when he wrote of his memories of working in Saskatchewan. He noted that Prairie society "seemed inextricably bound to the land it was based on, as Galt or Toronto or Lake Simcoe were not — the people were *of* the land" (*The Private Voice* 89). Landscape in the west provides the psychic resources from which a sense of personal identity may be developed. Although local lore and heritage are rich here, too, history does not confront westerners daily in the form of buildings, artefacts, and monuments. (Could this attention to the life of the community, rather than to the narrative of history, help explain why visitors to western Canada often refer to their hosts as being particularly "friendly"?)

Those who move away from these Ontario cities can return and find that their "home town" may have grown, but the core remains in many cases intact. That is certainly the case with the Galt that Gzowski knew.

When, as the celebrated host of *Morningside*, Gzowski returned to his home town, the Kitchener-Waterloo *Record* was there to capture the event on film. One of the things he did was to stand in the front yard of his childhood home in Galt, 24 Park Avenue. As he said in a conversation later, the noise of Cambridge that day was the main sensual event to be savoured:

It was really *nice* to be there. The sounds were very evocative, the sound of standing in front of 24 Park Avenue. I don't even know if it was a ghost sound or not: it was the train. The railroad bridge is within your eyeline from the front yard. The bridge is across the river, where we used to walk over illegally to the Galt Collegiate Institute. I could hear the train. ("Interview," 1992 [Adria])

The quotation represents a vivid recollection of a contemplative moment. At Gzowski's mention of the phantom train of today and the memory of the sensuous sound of the train of his childhood, we may speculate on the calming, insular feeling to be experienced in any community that has a river in its heart and a train coursing through its environs.

The centre of activity for Peter in winter was the skating rink in Dickson Park. As he would recall in *The Game of Our Lives*, the preparations leading up to the beginning of the season were themselves a kind of ritual for the city:

Even before freeze-up, workmen would set up boards around the rink's space, and the boards would stand there through the last days of autumn, pale against the darkening grass, waiting for the season to begin. Metal light standards sprouted along their edges. With the first frost, the workmen would begin to flood, so that well before Christmas we could skate, and each day after school and all day on weekends, until spring softened the ice, we would give our lives to our game. (79)

When he talks about these memories and others connected to his upbringing in Galt, Gzowski states that he intends to reflect extensively on them someday in preparation for some publishing project of the future:

I want to plant myself there and write about it. It's very evocative for me to be there. . . . It was a wonderful place to grow up. It's right out of Norman Rockwell, through a Canadian lens. It was in my view the perfect sized community to grow up in. ("Interview," 1992 [Adria])

The Browns' home was the upper half of a pleasant brick duplex (figures 6) overlooking Dickson Park. The building was a single-family dwelling both before and after their residence there. Park Avenue is still the peaceful enclave it was when Gzowski was a boy. It is easy to see how growing up in a town like Galt would affect your view of the world later. In such a town, community cohesiveness was nurtured through a common recognition of social roles. In Galt, for example, as in so many other southern Ontario towns, the business owner was your neighbour. This was emphasized by his proximity to you as a resident of the town but also by the indigenous nature of industry. In Galt, the industry was knitting, and those who ran that industry lived in the town and participated in the town's civic activities. Commerce, civility, and citizenship did not have to be inculcated in school — although they were anyway — since these were the qualities of community life that were enlivened in one's daily activities. The city's motto is "Progress through unity."

All community activities in such a city were connected. Civic administration was informed by the principles animated by church and enterprise; entertainment and recreation were intended to reinforce one's fitness for citizenship; the benevolent campaigns were directed by prominent business owners. Perhaps not surprisingly, Gzowski was to look for family and social "connections" in Canadian society throughout his life, a tendency that would find its culmination in the publication of his book *An Unbroken Line*. Beyond that expression of civic duty, however, was the common understanding that for the good of the community, certain things, even if important and apparent to most people, should go unstated; certain things that were of less importance should be repeated often. If the business owner was a member of the community, as he invariably was, he deserved your respect. This is not to say that in such a town a person must be less frank than a person in a large city, only that the social bonds that ensure the survival of any community — large city or small town — are more exposed to scrutiny in a smaller population. Conversational convention follows.

It was a small-town upbringing and it was a British upbringing. As he was to write in *The Private Voice*, the Union Jack and the

Crown were ubiquitous symbols of tradition and civility to a much greater extent than they are now:

> Like everyone else who was born in English Canada when I was, or who came here as a child, I was schooled to be British. (69).

The schooling to which he refers is the education he received not only at public school, Galt Collegiate, which he attended until 1949, but also at Ridley College, the private school he attended for three years thereafter. And the connection between Gzowski's upbringing and the sensibility he has taken to his broadcasting and writing career is one that he himself has made explicit in *The New Morningside Papers*:

> Maybe *The Morningside Papers*, new this season, still newer and even more expanded in seasons to come, ought to be a regular event, a grown-up Canadian version of the British children's annuals I remember from my childhood. (15)

As he was to note elsewhere, the British annuals included for young Peter *Chums* and *The Boy's Own Annual* (*The Private Voice* 69).

Reflecting the influence of the Empire and, perhaps, that of the small town, the habit of addressing men older than himself as *sir* was instilled in Galt. This was something that most schoolboys at the time would have learned. However, for Gzowski the practice has never really withered; he says that in personal interactions he maintains the habit. As well, in his radio conversations there is still something of the deference to the key members of the community — if not to the business owners of Galt, then to national or regional political leaders. One part of Gzowski's world-view, which was developed in the British tones of a Canadian small town, is that social unity is an ideal that can be approximated through artful conversation — through saying some things and leaving some things unsaid.

Gzowski himself ("Interview," 1992 [Adria]) has touched on this point, when he has discussed the differences between his work on *90 Minutes Live* and that on *Morningside*, referring to "certain lies of omission" that occur on the later show. An example he provides is the fact that on his list of ten favourite things (a kind of game on *Morningside*, which had listeners mailing in their own lists), Scotch whisky was left off, while warm socks and the like made the cut.

The connection between social graces on the one hand and, on the other, notions of the Canadian identity is a close one. For Peter growing up in Galt, a sense of politesse was instilled, which in his middle age he would identify as a defining characteristic of Canadian society:

> I think we're a polite people, I mean "have been." I think it's a national characteristic, compared to Americans, not compared to Japanese, not compared to Brits. ("Interview," 1992 [Adria])

Decorum, the scrupulous observance of generally accepted codes of social behaviour, characterizes an advanced culture. Peter's family heritage, which he could trace back to a great-great-grandfather and beyond, was a reminder that Canadians had reached such a stage of refinement. The nineteenth century had been an era of Romantic art, the dream of a marriage of industry and culture, the cultivation for the middle and upper classes of belles-lettres. In childhood, Peter had mastered that other carry-over from another century, "artful conversation," which he was to display in his broadcasting career. Such communion can occur only in a social context in which the participants have agreed upon the fundamental values that inform the culture.

When, on *Morningside*, Gzowski carries out an interview with the premier of Quebec in a tone some consider to be obsequious, he is retrieving a core feature of his upbringing in Galt. The interview is for Gzowski an interchange in which the participants have agreed on the essential terms of the society's cohesion. There is room, of course, for varying opinions and even simple disagreement. But Gzowski's sense of "Canadian politesse" forbids a fundamental challenge to the other's point of view. To do so would be to allow that a strand of the social web has separated. In the *Morningside* books, Gzowski writes persuasively, even passionately, about the place that French Quebec has and should have in the Canadian fabric. Face to face, in the studio, he does not take as firm a position. In conversation, he will never stray beyond the bounds of a social world in which one greets one's seniors by the appropriate form of address.

THE ROAD TO RIDLEY

As he grew up, Peter learned to golf. He skated and played hockey. He spent summers at his paternal grandparents' cottage at Lake Simcoe, fifty miles from Toronto, and at Nagiwa, a rugged boys' camp on the Severn River. During his teenage years, Peter went to Toronto on weekends to visit his grandparents — the same ones who had provided solace and shelter at the time of Margaret and Harold's estrangement — who lived in the top floor of 39 Rosehill Avenue. Sometimes he stayed with his father, who was living at a bootlegger's house at 32 Tranby, just off Avenue Road. His father had spent the years since Peter's birth, which included the end of the Depression and World War II, wandering the world, playing bridge obsessively, picking grapefruits in the southern United States, and finding, in England, another wife, Brenda Raikes, whom he married in 1940.

Peter heard other things about his father's activities. Harold also apparently worked during these years as a miner in Red Lake, Ontario, and a reporter in New Orleans. The bootlegger in whose house Harold lived was Jimmy Drope, the covert, but famous nonetheless, supplier of spirits to Toronto's upper-middle-class households. When in Toronto, Harold occupied the top two floors of Drope's house. In spite of the complicated circumstances of her husband's life, Margaret never spoke ill of Harold in Peter's presence.

Peter's relationship with his natural father would always be ambivalent. In his paternal ancestry, Peter found the civility and kindness of his grandfather and the traces of the accomplishments of Sir Casimir. But his father was enigmatically distant, both emotionally and geographically, for most of his son's youth and young adulthood. Peter would suggest in his later recollections that he would never resolve for himself this contradiction:

> My father, the family black sheep who had little to do with raising me but who was good company when he stopped by, interrupted his social life long enough to teach me, along with the secrets of garlic spaghetti sauce and where to get a shoeshine, how to read the *Racing Form* — which may, come to think of it, be legacy enough. (*An Unbroken Line* 170)

The two were not strangers, but neither were they intimate as father and son ("Interview," 1992 [Adria]). Communication between the two was strained and infrequent. Poignantly, the broadcaster who was to become famous for his long conversations on radio and for his public reinvention (through the *Morningside* books) of the pastime of letter-writing scarcely had contact, directly or indirectly, with his own father:

> He was really likeable. He would be funny and charming with me, but we didn't ever have a long talk, ever, about anything. . . . I probably had three letters from him in my life and probably wrote him two.

If Harold Gzowski's attention was a dappled offering for young Peter, the situation with his stepfather was easier to comprehend. Peter seemed neither to like nor dislike the man whom his mother had married. He would simply refrain from investing much interest or affection in Reg Brown. Instead, he looked to the Gzowski family history for an affirmation of his

P.B. LE PAGE, R.F. HODGINS, P.J. GZOWSKI, J.K. CONKLIN,
(ALTERNATE) (ALTERNATE) (ALTERNATE) (ALTERNATE)

FIGURE 7

Peter (second from right) on the
Ridley College football team (1950).

identity, receiving letters from his paternal grandmother that were addressed to *Peter John Gzowski Brown*. The family heritage would remain imprinted in Peter's consciousness because of the visits to his grandparents in Toronto.

The visits to Toronto were therapeutic for Peter, because he could learn, from his grandparents and sometimes from his father himself, of how his father was doing. But the visits were also painful, because some of his father's pursuits were naturally puzzling for the boy. One of Peter's visits to Toronto was during the Christmas of 1949, when he was fifteen, halfway through Grade 11, or third form, as it was called then. Peter must have expressed something to his father of his anguish at home, for as a result of their meeting, the elder Gzowski decided to enroll his son at Ridley College, a private school for boys in St. Catharines. Peter returned home only to gather his clothes. He changed his name back to Gzowski.

Ridley was the influence from his adolescence that more than anything instilled in Peter a sense of direction and discipline. In a *Maclean's* article published in 1961 entitled, "My First Negro," in which he used the pseudonym St. Edward's to refer to Ridley, Gzowski wrote that the school modelled itself on the English system and that the students' parents fell into one of the following categories: they were wealthy and wanted the prestige that a private school offered; they were "old boys" of the school or clergymen, both groups whose members received a discount on tuition; they travelled a great deal and needed the convenience of a boarding school; or they were Americans or South Americans who wanted the rigours of an English school for their son but settled for a Canadian version of such a school.

Ridley was élitist by definition, and, like other institutions of the day, it had an ambivalent attitude towards non-whites and non-Christians. In the same article, Gzowski writes that St. Edward's

was the kind of school that might have accepted a Negro from Brooklyn just *because* he was a Negro, as long as he was the only one. There was a Jew there, the year behind me. (66)

Gzowski has said that, "Ridley whipped me into shape" (Abley 23). The school called for discipline in all areas of a boy's life, including dress. It seems that it also offered to young Peter a proving ground for the amusements he was to pursue later in life: smoking, betting on sports, drinking. Gzowski described the three of them in some detail in "My First Negro." From his first day at the school, for example, the rituals of personal hygiene were combined with rituals of another kind:

> That first morning had been all strangeness to me, from the act of brushing my teeth with eight other boys lined up like grinning Rockettes before a mirror, to having to sneak into a gully behind our dormitory to have a cigarette — I hadn't yet learned to call it a "butt" — between breakfast and chapel. (30)

For another example, here is a description of a particularly memorable night of distraction during the Ridley academic year:

> Everyone in the class took his monthly leave the same Friday evening. We chartered a bus and went to a nearby town where we could drink. We came back late, broke and singing or broke and sick, but full of beer and satisfaction and comradeship. (67)

Significantly, it was his father and grandfather (the eldest Gzowski paying the bills) who arranged for Gzowski to attend, rescuing him from a juvenile state of emotional paralysis. But while Harold Gzowski's action was laudable, it was perhaps too late. For Peter had spent most of the years of his childhood without his natural father, and this seems to have been cause for emotional pain for the boy. Ridley was to instil in Peter the sense of fraternal affection that his father and grandfather perhaps wished for him. But there was an emotional space, which connected to his relationships with other men, about which Peter was to remain anxious throughout his life. As an adult, he would name as heroes Paul Hiebert and W.O. Mitchell, men who had taken him by the arm or modelled the characteristics of fatherhood that Peter imagined as idyllic. The most often-cited hero was to be Ralph Allen, a mentor he would meet at *Maclean's* magazine, whose death Peter would publicly and repeatedly mourn.

LEGACY OF A NATION-BUILDER

Though Harold Gzowski was absent for virtually all of his son's childhood and youth, the Gzowski patrimony, his forefathers' heritage, was a manifest element of Peter's education. He wrote about his consciousness of the Gzowski name in an article when he was twenty-four years old:

> I estimate that three thousand times during my six years as a working journalist, I have had to leave my name with a secretary or switchboard girl. On two thousand, nine hundred and ninety-seven of those occasions I have been forced to spell my name . . . Yet this difficult-to-pronounce, impossible-to-spell, and now-all-but-forgotten name was once as well known — and as important — in Canada as any of the legions of Mac's, Mc's, O's, 'sons and occasional 'bakers that now swell our archives, ring through Hansard and shine from brass plaques in a thousand grey public buildings. ("What It's Like" 24)

Sir Casimir Gzowski, the first Gzowski to live in North America and Peter's great-great-grandfather, was the main theme in the family story. Sir Casimir was a Polish émigré who in Canada specialized in championing and building up public works. Born

37

March 5, 1813, in St. Petersburg, he was the son of a diplomat and military officer. Unusually tall and with a commanding demeanour (not unlike the stature of his famous great-great-grandson), Sir Casimir was involved in the Polish uprisings of 1830 and 1831 against the Russian government. As a result of these and other activities, he fled with fellow Polish nationalists to New York, where he arrived in March 1834. His training in Poland had been in engineering, and this was the field in which he would contribute to Canadian life. However — and this is an indication of his aptitude for hard work and application, which was to be passed on to Peter — he was admitted to the Bar in the State of Pennsylvania in 1837.

On assignment from the engineering firm for which he worked in Pennsylvania, Gzowski went to St. Catharines to obtain business for the firm. When his work took him to Kingston, he was called upon by the Governor of Canada, Sir Charles Bagot. According to a biography of Sir Casimir, Sir Charles was so impressed by Gzowski that he insisted the engineer be kept in Canada. Gzowski moved to Canada in 1841, where he took on the duties of Superintendent of Roads and Waterways in the London District of Upper Canada.

Sir Casimir's professional callings were engineer and lawyer. But his enthusiasms were always directed at strengthening the Canadian infrastructure. And in this we find yet another similarity with his great-great-grandson, since Peter was to make the enhancement of the Canadian identity one of his main concerns as a broadcaster. Sir Casimir paved Yonge Street (which at the time connected Toronto, Lake Simcoe, Georgian Bay, and the northern sections of Ontario) and founded Wycliffe College. He was involved in exploring for mining deposits in northern Ontario and in planning and building railroads in Quebec. He worked on the Montreal harbour and the Toronto waterfront, built the bridge across the Niagara River between Buffalo and Fort Erie, and completed surveys of the inland water systems of Ontario, Quebec, New Brunswick, and Nova Scotia. He died August 24, 1898, at the age of eighty-five years.

A historical footnote concerning Sir Casimir connects in a curiously direct way to Peter's life. Sir John A. Macdonald wrote to him in November 1870, asking him to be on the Canadian Canal Commission, the body that was first to envision the Great Lakes navigation system as a whole, "from the western end at Fort William and Duluth on Lake Superior to its eastern terminus in Montreal." In the letter, Sir John stated the following about the Commission:

> The object, as you know, is not a mere engineering one, but one to consider the comparative importance of our various lines of water communications and the best means of improving such communications as a whole. . . . (Kos-Rabcewicz-Zubkowski 106)

Sir John evidently had great confidence in Gzowski's ability to contribute to the development of Canada's "communications." These communications would be the means by which Canadian society might cohere. Of course, more than one hundred years later, Peter's public role would be lauded as contributing to Canada's communications, as well. Peter would write about his consciousness of Sir Casimir's influence when he worked for *Maclean's* magazine in the 1960s. The knowledge of Sir Casimir's "communications" helped form a template in which Peter could establish his own career in communications. The artefacts of both men's efforts — landmarks on the one hand and books on the other — would be different, but the ends would be the same.

CHANNELS OF IDENTITY

In considering the relationship of Peter Gzowski with his illustrious great-great-grandfather, we may discern further the development of Peter's private mythology. On the one hand, Peter has described the importance in his formative years of the intimate, resonating space of radio within which he, like so many of his generation, found psychic shelter. He has written that when ill as a child, he was allowed to take the kitchen radio to bed for comfort. As he cradled the set in his arms, the adventures of American heroes and anti-heroes must have provided a strange assurance of a well-ordered society. As well, the newspaper provided a different kind of space, one in which the social protection of the community could be reinforced. Here, the outrageous dramas being played out on foreign stages were set in counterpoint to the solid, friendly patronage and public concern of the merchants and politicians of Galt.

On the other hand, Peter was sensitive to the conflict between the cultural expression he heard on radio — largely American — and the cultural environment he saw. The aural contradicted the visual for him, and his powers of apprehension were compelling enough — as we have learned from the accomplishments of his subsequent career — to cause him to seek resolution. That search is in evidence in all of his professional efforts since then, but most singularly in *Morningside*.

But this notion must be pressed further. Not only must Gzowski have felt that radio's American cultural content clashed with what he viewed as Canada's cultural context, but it clashed also with his family's mythology, and thereby with his own identity, which included a sense of lineage from Sir Casimir. For the great public works of Sir Casimir — whose portrait hung in the living room of Peter's paternal grandfather — were part of a project to strengthen not North America but *British* North America, life as it is lived in the northerly parts of the continent. Sir Casimir was honoured for his erection of public works, but he also called for the preservation of those works: his reputation is founded as much on his advocacy for military preparedness as it is on development. For Canada in the nineteenth century, of course, the main object of defence was to check the territorial ambitions of the United States.

Paradoxically, though Gzowski has commented that as a child he was "schooled to be British," he has also said that he was "growing up American" ("Interview," 1992 [Adria]). The influence of the school was contradicted daily by the influence of

FIGURE 9

Four generations of Gzowski men on Christmas Eve, 1960: Peter with,
from the left, his father (Harold Edward Gzowski), paternal grandfather
(Harold Northey Gzowski), and son (Peter Casimir Gzowski).

PHOTO COURTESY OF SIMON BURKE AND MAGRELYS RODRIGUES

media. The school taught him about social connections and graces; radio and newspapers taught him about action and enterprise. The tension between the American model and the British / Canadian variation was to become evident in Gzowski's approach to newspaper reporting, magazine writing, radio broadcasting, and sports writing. The Canadian version was for Gzowski more rooted in the written word. While he would eventually embrace radio and television, the "new media," radio, with its intimations of the "writer-speaker" (Marshall McLuhan's term), was to become his best love.

If Gzowski was influenced by having grown up in a small southern Ontario town, we can assume that this upbringing might, like the importance of the influence of Sir Casimir's legacy, help us to understand the way he thinks about the world and about his country. For Gzowski, Canada's social structure is commensurable with, I would venture, that of a small town. The communication channels in such a town — in the 1940s and 1950s, newspapers and radio — might help reveal the patterns by which Gzowski, like other residents of such communities, organized his perceptions and formed his conclusions about the nature of society.

Young Gzowski was a carrier for the Galt *Daily Reporter*, as he was for the London *Free Press*. The experience of delivering the *Reporter* evidently evokes vivid memories for Peter, as this quotation from *The Fourth Morningside Papers* suggests:

When, delivering the Galt *Reporter* along the snowbound streets, running a trapline in my mind, I shouted a silent "gee," the chimerical dog team fanning out ahead of me turned right as surely as my stepfather's Oldsmobile coupe did when he turned the wheel. (29)

As Peter was growing up, the *Daily Reporter* was a Thomson paper, as its successor, the Cambridge *Reporter*, is today. In the late 1940s, as now, it resembled its colleagues in the chain visually and stylistically. In 1948, the paper was twenty pages in length, no longer than the typical length of its modern counterpart. It sold for twenty-four cents a week or twelve dollars a year. It appeared every afternoon except Sunday. In 1948, when Gzowski was at the mature paper-delivering age of fourteen, the paper consistently featured international news on the front page: "United Kingdom Will Pay Higher Prices for Farm Products from Canada." (Today, the story might be "Canada Gets Tough with Serbia.") But there was always a mix in the length and scope of the stories. The local and regional news was never ignored. One story in January that year began, "Births in Brantford in 1947 set a new high of 1,500." As I will discuss, *Morningside*, too, provides a perspective on the world for the benefit of its audience. Delivered daily, accessible, current: the radio show, like the newspaper the young Peter delivered, presents current events for easy consumption.

The ads were prominent in such a paper. In Galt, Briscoe's, a clothier, might have an overcoat sale. Again, the merchants were citizens and neighbours, and for Gzowski this relationship seems to have had a lasting effect on his view of society. The merchants' ads were placed for the purpose of promoting their wares, but the revenue from such promotion subsidized the presentation of news and information. On Saturday, the ads might include a promotion for a movie being shown in town, perhaps featuring Gene Kelly or another American star. Royal gossip, recipes, radio listings, and sports were topics worthy of publication. There was a humorous side to the paper and a corresponding serious side. Regular features were the "Wise Crack for Today" and an assortment of editorial cartoons reprinted from American newspapers; items might warn against the dangers of drinking alcohol or, turning to the subject of electrical power, state that "Live Wires Are Deadly." In short, the newspaper had a mix of items not unlike that of *Morningside*. For Gzowski, *Morningside* was to be a natural extension of the daily paper he had known in Galt. Both tried to appeal to the varying tastes of an aspiring, educated, conscientious middle class.

The paper was a total experience for the reader. It drew on the community's values, emotions, and sentiments. There was an ideological view to be presented in the *Reporter*, but like the civic duties for which it gave expression, that stance was implied, integrated with the events of daily life. The same edition of the paper that counselled sobriety ran the story "Pravda Says Life in U.S. Like That of Nazi Germany." The paper challenged the reader to consider the widest scope of social conditions, with its notices of the horrors that were occurring in other parts of the world. But it also made the reader feel as if the community provided protection against external forces. The message was that while there were some ugly things going on around the world and even within the community, the appropriate response was not fear or criticism but civic enterprise and participation. Again, for Gzowski the effect of this message was to be long-lasting. Later in his life, he would devote portions of his books, broadcasts, and periodical articles to his adopted cause, that of adult literacy. That wealth brings with it responsibility had been taught through the medium of the *Reporter*, and the message seems to have persisted for Gzowski.

So the newspaper was a channel by which the world was "delivered" to the home in Galt. Another channel was radio, but while the newspaper was a kind of relief map, showing the events of the world as a vivid backdrop for daily life in an apparently self-contained community, radio was a porthole through which the world could be viewed. Turning to the painting terminology of *figure* and *ground*, which Marshall McLuhan used frequently, for the newspaper reader the *figure* was the community (or perhaps the *figure* was the medium itself), the *ground* the world. For the radio listener, the roles were reversed.

Radio for those growing up in the 1930s and 1940s was the means by which American culture gained its strongest influence. Gzowski has written about the potency for the childhood imagination of such radio dramas as *The Shadow*, *Dragnet*, and *The Green Hornet*. One of the few broadcasts of Canadian origin was *Hockey Night in Canada*. Listeners of that generation would only gradually begin to associate an electric medium with the Canadian experience. The world through the porthole was associated with progress, the magic of technology, social order. It was not a version of the world, but an American dream. For Gzowski, however, that dream would eventually require an opposing Canadian version, something that in full development would sound very much like *Morningside.*

2. Newspaperman

MOVING ON

As I'm getting ready to leave after one of our interviews, Gzowski is fiddling with a yellow Post-it sticker on a copy of his best-selling book, *The Morningside Papers*. He seems restless and tired. The second volume of what is to become a series of *Morningside* books will be published shortly. After I leave, he will discuss the cover of the book with a graphic artist. During the rest of the day he will attend a meeting to plan his annual golf tournament for literacy and do background work on upcoming subjects for his radio program. The radio preparation includes watching a videotape of three Quebec feminist writers and reading a book on economics. He's been up since 4:00 a.m.; it's now 2:30 p.m. I'm outside his office when he mumbles *sotto voce*, so I'm the only one in the din of the *Morningside* offices who can hear him: "Don't call me Mr. Gzowski."

Gzowski works long hours in order to carry out the many roles he has taken on: broadcaster, advocate for the CBC, benefactor of the cause of literacy, golfer, magazine columnist, author and editor, family member, horse-racing enthusiast. In his daily activities, the social, professional, and personal lives of Peter Gzowski seem to merge. As testament to this, his personal assistant, who manages his activities and screens his callers and visitors, is paid half of her salary by the CBC and half by Gzowski personally. When she reads the many letters that Gzowski receives from his *Morningside* listeners, it is impossible to determine whether the duty flows from Gzowski's interest as an employee or as personal enterprise. Reading and answering a letter is, of course, related to the job as radio host. However, if the letter ends up in a *Morningside* book, there will be a personal financial interest in the activity.

As with other public figures, his schedule is filled many weeks and months in advance. His life is like a small industry, combining daily the pursuits of benevolence, profit-making, and personal promotion and development. He works intensively to keep the industry going. As if to formulate an antidote to his diagnosis of his natural father's essential failing — "booze and purposelessness," as he told Mark Abley (26) — Gzowski ensures that his days are filled with purpose, busy with activity, bristling with action and change. All of this is accomplished by maintaining a working day whose hours are more numerous than many people's waking day.

The restlessness and the long days were in evidence early in Gzowski's career. He has spent decades finishing one project and starting another, quitting a job to take a more promising one, perpetually moving on. Journalism provided for Gzowski an opportunity to mould a career around his wandering while also allowing him to explore certain connections in the Canadian social fabric. For a journalist, having something to "do," something to report on, is a prerequisite for working. When, occasionally, the treadmill has stopped for Gzowski (as it did, for example, when his television show, *90 Minutes Live*, came to an abrupt end in 1978), he claims that he has nothing to write about. The hectic pace of journalism gives him an incentive to overcome what he himself calls his tendency towards laziness. According to Gzowski, what is common to all the journalistic jobs he has held is that he "finds out about something and then tells others" ("Interview," 1987 [Adria]).

This sense of journalistic busy-work is not shared by all journalists, of course. His daughter Alison, who has written a book about the cultural and economic changes taking place in eastern Europe as they are affecting youth, apparently felt insulted when Gzowski suggested that she write about a topic in which she had no interest. Responding to his daughter's search for another

47

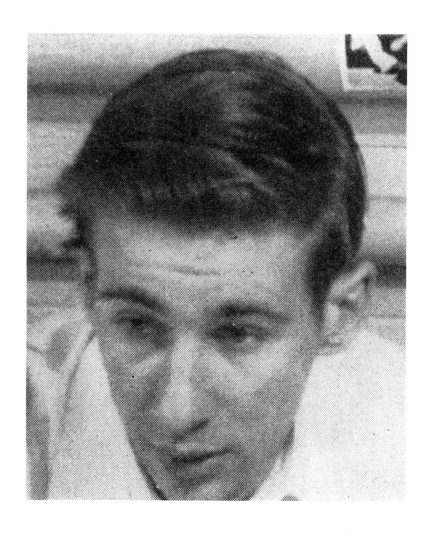

FIGURE 10

Editor of the University of Toronto Varsity *newspaper.*
PHOTO COURTESY UNIVERSITY OF TORONTO ARCHIVES

project, he had suggested that she travel with and write about a rock band on the ascent to stardom ("Interview," 1992 [Adria]), a proposal that she "spit back." The incident illustrates the difference in perspective that Gzowski has with other journalists and writers. He finds just about anything culturally interesting; as a young journalist he took up the challenges as they came.

In the twenty years or so that followed his departure from Ridley College in 1952, Gzowski spent most of his creative energy writing and editing. In 1954, he got his first newspaper job at the Timmins *Daily Press* where, based in the town of Kapuskasing, he used his post as advertising salesman as a pretext for filing stories for the paper. The *Daily Press* was famous in Canada because it was the first newspaper Roy Thomson owned. It was a kind of training ground for other journalists who would later enjoy a national reputation.

In 1955, Gzowski was appointed police reporter at the Toronto *Telegram*. He interrupted his career as a reporter twice in the 1950s to attend classes at the University of Toronto, but even his studies were punctuated by journalistic enterprise. For the academic years beginning in September of 1955 and 1956, he held the elected position of editor of the University of Toronto *Varsity*. Studying and "newspapering" made up only a part of the university experience for Peter:

> In my day, the climax of the football weekend was the Saturday evening party on St. George Street. I mean party, singular, because everyone moved from fraternity house to fraternity house, using only the flimsiest of acquaintance-ships to get in. ("The Raffish Tradition" 36)

While a university student, Gzowski met Robert Fulford, who in 1968 would be appointed editor of *Saturday Night* magazine, in the press room at police headquarters. The two worked the night shift for the police beat, Gzowski for the Toronto *Telegram*, Fulford for the *Globe*. Fulford once noticed during the course of the evening that Gzowski had in his possession a book by John

FIGURE II

Peter pours from a jeroboam of champagne in celebration
of his last day at Maclean's *magazine, September 4, 1964.*
Robert Fulford stands next to Peter.

PHOTO COURTESY OF PETER GZOWSKI

Milton. Fulford asked if he liked it. Gzowski replied, "Hello, no. I'm a Joe College. It's on the course." According to Fulford, Gzowski was affecting an attitude of nonchalance about his literary interests and "already dreamt of being considered just one of the guys" (58).

It was true that Gzowski tried to cover any pretensions at intellectual refinement during his days at university. This attitude towards a "life of the mind" can be discerned today. He expresses difficulty, for example, in discussing poetry with his guests on air. With his university friends Gzowski would use the nickname "Publius Maximus" for a particularly gifted student of Latin and English, preferring to learn how to read the *Racing Form* to the set texts:

> I learned how to conjugate the verb "to win" in racetrack-ese: I win, you win, he win, they win, whatever the tense or mood — he win big yesterday, he win big today and he win even bigger tomorrow. (*An Unbroken Line* 170)

Gzowski did not seem to see a need to finish his degree. His future lay in the world of journalism, in which he had already gained experience through his work on the *Daily Press*, the *Telegram*, and the *Varsity*. His degree has remained unfinished, although in his middle age several universities have conferred on him academic distinctions in recognition of his life accomplishments as a journalist and public figure.

When classes were finished in 1957, Gzowski got on a train for Moose Jaw, where he took a job as the city editor at the *Times-Herald*. Almost every year during the 1950s, then, Gzowski was in a new job, in a strange city or town, facing a fresh challenge. During that decade, he was variously a university student, an advertising salesman, a reporter in Timmins, Moose Jaw, Chatham, and Toronto, and an editor at both a student newspaper and a national magazine. The process of continually moving on did not end until his association with *Morningside*. Not surprisingly, the professional restlessness suggested by these moves is echoed by Gzowski's personal presence. In conversation he is extraordinarily attentive to the other person; moments before the conversation formally ends, however, he is already reading something else, his back turned, contemplating the next task to be completed, fiddling with the next Post-it note.

Part of Gzowski's inclination to work constantly and intensively is related to what Fulford regards as a competitive nature. Fulford has noted that Gzowski has always liked to add a competitive twist to both personal and professional activities. When the two were playing checkers once in a bar in Regina, Fulford began winning the game. Then, finding himself distracted, Fulford suggested they stop playing. Gzowski responded in a way that revealed his apparent need to play at all times to win:

> Don't do that, Fulford. This may be the only game in the world that you can beat me at. Make the most of it. (Fulford 145–46)

As a result of this abundance of competitive energy directed early at advancing his career, Gzowski was later to reflect on what he might have missed in the doing. While he worked as a journalist in small Canadian cities as a young man, many of his contemporaries were travelling abroad, experimenting with the personal implications of a wealthier postwar North American society, as he wrote in *An Unbroken Line*:

> After university, when most of my contemporaries... went to London or Paris or Zagreb, I went to Moose Jaw, Saskatchewan, to learn about newspapers. . . . (171)

When he was established as a writer at the age of thirty-five and finally able to travel for personal or professional reasons, Gzowski was to conclude that such journeys could only confirm that he had not really missed much. New York or London or Russia could only be themselves, he mused, and the conclusion he made after travelling was, "I have never yet been what I want to be: *surprised*" ("The Global Village" 33).

Energetic accomplishment has always been Gzowski's mode of existence. Like Fulford, Gzowski has rarely had only one occupation at a time. Even while a student at university, he worked at the *Telegram* and then the *Varsity*. More recently, while the industries of *Morningside* — books, publicity, the program itself — churn, Gzowski continues to write for a national magazine on the side; in the mid-1980s he juggled the duties of host of both radio and television. Looking back on such a life, as he does occasionally, he does not regret the loss that has accompanied it. The next accomplishment is too much on his mind.

The constant activity is reflected in his countenance. I remember seeing a photograph of him in the newspaper, accompanying an article publicizing his tour in support of *The New Morningside Papers*. He must have just wakened, opened his hotel room door to the reporter, and started the interview. He looked haggard. When I met him in 1992, he looked pitifully run down. That day his left eye was swollen almost shut. His voice was hoarse, the skin on his face inflamed. After a few moments, however, he became the Gzowski heard on radio: articulate, amiable, thoughtful. During our conversation, he said that he always felt exhausted at the end of a radio season.

MAKING CONNECTIONS

During the 1950s and 1960s, Gzowski worked in two cities outside southern Ontario: Timmins, Ontario, and Moose Jaw, Saskatchewan. These cities were to confirm his social sensibility, which I will describe as "romantic traditionalist." If Galt helped form Gzowski's conception of social relations, Timmins and Moose Jaw shaped his view of Canada's regions; they were the first influences on the development of his ideal of Canadian unity.

Timmins and Moose Jaw gave Gzowski intellectual pegs on which he could hang his notions of the northerly and westerly regions of Canada. Of course, it is impossible to understand completely the sensibility of the people who live in a locale by simply taking up residence for several months. However, as was to become evident in his career, the waves of empathy and sympathy he now sets in motion through broadcasting — the power he has to make people say he "really listens" — have been made possible by just such sojourns. After his jobs at the *Daily Press* and the *Times-Herald*, Gzowski would imply he could imagine what daily life might be for people other than those living in southern Ontario. He married a woman from the Prairies. Romantically, he was to write later that people on the Prairies were connected to their landscape in a way he had not considered before:

> The prairie . . . was civilized. Yet that civilization seemed inextricably bound to the land it was based on, as Galt or Toronto or Lake Simcoe were not — the people were *of* the land. The men I met, outside the newspaper office, had powerful hands, sun-dark faces with white foreheads, and indelible memories of the dust that had drifted over Moose Jaw less than twenty years before. The women were stoic and strong. (*The Private Voice* 89)

The experience of observing landscape was to have resonances later in his life. For example, in "Whistling Down the Northern Lights," an essay he published in *The Fourth Morningside Papers*, he would write with simple passion about the size and sweep of the Canadian north:

> Know something? Canada, which we tend to think of as a thin ribbon of city lights stretched out along the forty-ninth parallel, is as high as it is wide. It's as far from Eureka, on Ellesmere Island, to Point Pelee in Ontario (which in fact is south of parts of California) as from Carbonear to Skidegate. The north is *enormous*. More than a third of our land mass lies above 60, and it's as varied — from mountains to deserts to icy archipelagos — as the rest of the country put together. . . . If we are bounded by the United States to the south, the

Pacific to the west and the Atlantic to the east, to the north there is only space. From the corner of Bloor and Spadina, if you wanted to and had five or six months to spare, you could walk to the North Pole. (30)

The time he spent in Timmins and Moose Jaw also contributed to Gzowski's "romantic traditionalist" sensibility. The two cities are cited by Gzowski as an influence on his stance as a journalist. He would imaginatively return to them throughout his career, as the quotation about the "stoic and strong" women suggests. Second, it was during his years as a junior journalist that Gzowski began renewing his interest in his family origins. As we saw when we visited Galt, Sir Casimir represented an important family connection for Gzowski. While Peter has mentioned publicly his mother's family and her descent from John A. Macdonald, most often he defines his heritage in terms of the Gzowski line, represented by the four generations of men of his lifetime. These four generations are represented in a photo taken on Christmas Eve in 1956 (figure 9). The photo shows the familial line that has become especially important to Gzowski.

The sign of the romantic traditionalist is that he or she sees importance in continually making connections in the social fabric. Such people are interested in discerning family and social ties; they look for and encourage bonds between groups and individuals. As the journalist Charles Taylor (mentioned in Gzowski's book *An Unbroken Line*) puts it, they want to know "who your people are." When making significant decisions, romantic traditionalists look to the lessons of history and to the ideal of social cohesion for their guidance.

After Gzowski's time in Timmins and Moose Jaw in the 1950s, the regional and geographical connections could be extended alongside the familial ones. An example of his interest in combined familial and social connections may be found in an incident recounted in *The Private Voice*. According to the anecdote, Gzowski is in The Double Hook bookstore in Montreal. He speculates, as an aside, on the reason his book *An Unbroken Line* is still being sold in that store. His speculation is based on his knowledge of the heritage, both historical and genealogical, of the proprietor. One of the owners of the store is, he points out, Judy Mappin, whose father was E.P. Taylor, "a hero of the race-track" (*The Private Voice* 294). (Journalist Charles Taylor is Judy's brother. The romantic traditionalist thrives on connections.)

Furthermore, Gzowski continues to refer to the "biggie" book he will write, or is writing, which will be, he emphasizes, a legacy for his kids. The romantic traditionalist imprint is not only on his concern that he leave something tangible for his children, but also on the technology he wants to use to accomplish that goal, that of the printed word. Writers are romantic traditionalists, working with an antique technology. They allude to other written works and other writers — without regard for time or contemporanaeity, as if it does not matter whether a writer is alive or has been dead for two hundred years. Writers assume a shared experience and a common heritage with their audience. "I'm a writer who's now working in radio," Gzowski says.

He feels that he has not yet written the book that will define his stature as a writer. The "biggie" book is being planned, but so is another, which will confirm his essential identity as a writer:

> I want to leave one good book behind me, and I haven't written it yet. I'm frustrated by my inability to get a book right. ("Interview," 1992 [Adria])

Gzowski's written contribution to the romantic traditional literature in Canada is *An Unbroken Line*. It has the seeds of the theme Gzowski really likes to pursue: the connection between his lineage and his personality. He compares the interconnections and lineages of thoroughbred horses to those of southern Ontario's oldest families — thus the title with its double meaning, referring to both equine and human ancestries. Here is an example of the kind of connection to be made in the book, this one about the artefacts of the racetrack:

On the west wall, high above the parimutuel machines, a plaque the size of a small barn door commemorates the winners of the Queen's Plate, a list that begins with Don Juan, which knocked off the third and final heat at the Carleton track in 1:58, June 27, 1860 — 122 years to the day before Son of Briartic — and ended, until Son of Briartic's victory, with Fiddle Dancer Boy, 1981, a mile and a quarter at Woodbine in 2:04.5.

But the human heritage is there, too, everywhere you turn. The burnished horn on which the call to the post is sounded for the Queen's Plate is the Hendrie horn, given by William Hendrie, an early president of the Jockey Club, to his grandson George Campbell Hendrie, a former managing editor, and now, in his late seventies, honorary president, and by George Hendrie to the club itself and its red-headed trumpeter Ed Pilar. (81–82)

In his personal and professional conversations, Gzowski repeatedly makes connections in the Canadian social fabric; in *An Unbroken Line* they are drawn in association with the "royal sport." The focal connection of the book: Sir Casimir himself, who in his senior years had been named an aide-de-camp to Queen Victoria, established the Queen's Plate in 1860.

Making connections is part of a collective effort for Gzowski. He seems to believe that he, like other Canadians, should have a part in defining or refining some notion of a "Canadian identity." Talking once to Murray McLauchlan, the singer-songwriter and a long-time acquaintance of Gzowski's, I asked whether the broadcaster was "searching for himself" through his efforts to articulate things Canadian. McLauchlan responded,

Probably. People do from time to time. We know what is *not* Canadian, but perhaps we don't know what *is*. We are not Americans, and we are not Japanese. We aren't supposed to be racist; we are supposed to be militant or apathetic. But in reality we are just a collection of human beings who happen to live in the same country . . . Canadians need to be shown themselves. They need heroes. (Adria 41)

Gzowski has been looking for heroes since his childhood, when he experienced the contradictory emotions of having "the family black sheep" for a father.

MARRIAGE

In the summer of 1957, while he was at the Moose Jaw *Times-Herald*, Gzowski met Jenny Lissaman, who worked as an interior designer for a firm of architects in Regina. The couple's first date was on Gzowski's twenty-third birthday. They were married in February 1958, just after Gzowski had moved back to Ontario to take the job of managing editor at the Chatham *Daily News*. The couple was to have five children, beginning with Peter Casimir, born later that year, who took the name of the family's illustrious ancestor. Alison, Maria, John, and Michael were born before 1965 had ended.

Gzowski has spoken and written of the dissolution of his marriage often. Those public statements are laid over a private anguish. While seemingly talking openly about his role in ending the relationship, Gzowski covers what must be the core of his true feelings. His communications on the subject are sometimes elliptical and ambiguous. In *The Private Voice*, he would write that,

What went wrong [in my marriage] is buried in what you already know about my life since then, and in the times. (40)

The marriage seemed tilted towards failure from the beginning. It brought together two people whose backgrounds would not lend themselves to harmony. Jenny's upbringing had been conservative, and she had been taught, like others of her generation in the west, the value of forbearance and reserve. He had

FIGURE 12

98 Lytton Boulevard, Toronto, purchased by the
Gzowskis in 1971, sold by Jenny Gzowski in the 1980s.
PHOTO COURTESY OF *MACLEAN'S*

emerged from an emotionally turbulent adolescence and had learned that immunity to personal pain could be purchased through a public articulation of his identity. When the uproar of family life was at a peak, Jenny kept to herself. During the same period, Peter was working long hours in an effort to define his professional and social lives, his personal life having been subsumed in the other two lives.

According to Gzowski, the couple didn't talk. For twenty years, two private spheres of activity simmered. Jenny's sphere was the hectic, continuous task of raising five children. Peter's was the desperate search for a private space within the professional and social space of media. (One strand of this search was the development of a personal attachment to Ralph Allen, editor of *Maclean's*.) Writing about a trip the couple took together in 1960, entitled, "Holiday Weekend in New York," Gzowski subtly revealed the disjunction between the two spheres when he referred to his wife's sleeping habits:

> Jennie, who is used to getting up at an unreasonable hour to feed and water babies, bounded from bed about seven to see our view. Twenty-two stories below, Central Park stretched to the north. . . . (32)

When the two spheres had run their course, the marriage ended. The social setting of the 1950s and 1960s did not provide much support for those who might have tried to find a meeting of the spheres. The ending, when it came in 1978, was to become, curiously, a source of some relief for Gzowski, as he recollected later in *The Private Voice*:

> The wounds have healed now, and the scar tissue is stronger than the original flesh. Life is better for us both. (43)

He still calls Jenny "my wife."

Gzowski has lived with Gillian Howard since 1983. The couple divide their time between Gzowski's condominium in down-

FIGURE 13

Peter, Jenny, and family at the Toronto Islands, 1972.
PHOTO COURTESY OF JOHN REEVES

town Toronto and a cottage adjoining the Briars golf club, at Jackson's Point, on Lake Simcoe near Sutton. Athletic and good-natured, Gillian plays golf with him on most weekends of the season. She also takes part in Gzowski's public, professional, and personal activities, from helping to organize the golf tournaments to which he has lent his name, to assisting with the compilation and editing of the *Morningside* books, to accompanying him to the horse-races, to which she brings her own particular interest. She is the eldest daughter of John and Nancy Howard, who have been prominent in the domain of Ontario horse-racing. She has been riding and watching horses since childhood. She has also been the assistant director of publicity at the Ontario Jockey Club. In fact, the two met during one of Gzowski's visits to the racetrack while he was writing *An Unbroken Line.*

MACLEAN'S

Gzowski began reading periodicals when he was a child, a time when devouring *The Boy's Own Annual* and *Chums* formed a staple of his leisure activities. Fancifully, he has suggested that the *Morningside* books could be published just as regularly, to form a kind of cultural digest for the nation (*The New Morningside Papers* 15). Among other periodicals he has written for, *Saturday Night* published articles of his after the early days at *Maclean's.*

The most controversial of these was the piece he wrote in May 1969 on the increasing frequency of the appearance in the popular media, at the time, of obscene words. ("You're just out of luck if it don't sound like — —," ventured the young writer ["How You Gonna" 31].) His interest in magazine writing continues to the present, with his regular columns in *Canadian Living* (now compiled in a book by the same title), which deal with more urbane topics than the one mentioned in *Saturday Night.* But *Maclean's* is the periodical to which Gzowski has directed most of his creative energy as a writer.

The first post Gzowski held at *Maclean's* was that of assistant editor, a job he took in 1958. *Maclean's* at that time was not the stylized news magazine it is today. With fewer publications with which to compete, an issue of *Maclean's* in 1958 allowed a writer to present his or her personality and views more directly than is possible today. Readers would become familiar with, for instance, Leslie Hannon's writing about the U.K. and would come to expect a particular literary style in association with the topic and the writer.

The magazine had at least one affinity with its cousin, the daily newspaper, with which Gzowski was familiar throughout his childhood in Galt. The editorial content and the advertising were linked quite openly. An article that appeared in January 1958 on "The Brave New World of Trailer Living" (by Christina McCall) would be followed by an advertisement the next month with the following copy: *A New Way of Life. Thousands each year are discovering the many advantages of living in a Mobile Home . . .*

Gzowski learned much about the craft of journalism from Ralph Allen, the editor of *Maclean's*, as did the other journeyman writers with whom Gzowski worked. In the words of Pierre Berton, who also worked there at the time, *Maclean's* was "a school of writing with Ralph Allen as the faculty" (*The Private Voice* 103). The path a story followed to publication in the magazine was an arduous one. An outline was prepared by the writer, which was then critiqued by three or four different sub-editors. By the time the outline reached Allen, many changes had been made, but he still offered blunt advice. The draft itself would go up the editorial line and back down to the author in the same way.

As a result, Gzowski learned early the value of researching, checking facts, and rewriting. He also developed a great affection for the older man. In Allen, Gzowski found the paternal example he felt he had missed in childhood. Allen displayed the qualities Gzowski considered to be exemplary: dedication, professionalism, discipline. Gzowski would not forget Allen's example. Two decades after Allen died, Gzowski would write and speak about him as he would a father, as we see in this quotation from *The Private Voice*:

I cannot write a paragraph or consider how to cover a story without thinking he might be looking over my shoulder, trying to make sure I do it as well as I can. (109)

According to Robert Fulford, Gzowski's articles during his years at *Maclean's* have withstood the test of time and still read well today. But as an editor at the age of twenty-eight, Gzowski found that the competitive spirit that helped to open up personal and professional opportunities did not necessarily make the duties of managing older and more experienced writers easier to carry out. Gzowski did not consider his youth to be a barrier to his responsibilities. Later, he was to report that he was, at the time, "a traffic craftsman" but also "a hotshot, and probably an objectionable one" (Abley 23). His staff frequently "found dealing with him uncomfortable" (Fulford 145).

Gzowski wrote a feature article every other issue or so in *Maclean's*, which appeared every two weeks. The magazine allowed Gzowski to nurture and express his advocacy of Canadian nationalism in a way that had not been possible during the years he spent at daily newspapers. Two artefacts from the time are testament to Gzowski's interest in promoting Canadian culture. The first is a book of essays on Canadian sports heroes that he wrote with Trent Frayne, the Toronto sports writer, entitled *Great Canadian Sports Stories: A Century of Competition*. Frayne wrote the prologue to the book and Gzowski the epilogue; between these pieces they each wrote several pieces on well-known Canadian athletes and sports figures. The book reveals Gzowski's long-time interest in sports, an interest that would lead, for example, to a sustained examination of the Edmonton Oilers in the late 1970s and a book on the topic published in 1981.

Gzowski's contributions to the book written with Frayne included profiles of Bob Hayward, a racing boat driver, Red Storey, the football player, and the boxer Louis Cyr. The book is

FIGURE 14

PHOTO COURTESY OF HOWARD WHYTE PHOTOGRAPHY

also testament to Gzowski's interest in things nationalistic. The book was published in anticipation of Canada's centennial year. Like other books published during that period, it celebrated Canada's history and culture. Gzowski's epilogue discussed what he called the "new age of amateurism" in Canadian sport, an era in which Canadians would participate more in physical activity and spectate less. The age apparently did not fulfil its early promise, but Gzowski's interest in a form of Canadian renaissance is something that he would continue to pursue in his later journalistic efforts.

The second testimonial to Gzowski's nationalistic sentiment in the mid-sixties was connected to the bicultural fact in Canada. After he was appointed Quebec editor of *Maclean's* in 1961, he took the opportunity to try to live and work in French, even to the point of moving in with a French-speaking family for a couple of weeks with the intention of experiencing firsthand some of the subtleties of French-Canadian culture. As with his stints in Timmins and Moose Jaw, the experience in Quebec lingered in his journalistic efforts. In the same year *Great Canadian Sports Stories* was published, a song co-written by "Pete" Gzowski and Ian Tyson was released on Ian and Sylvia's best-selling album *Early Morning Rain*. It was the album that was to introduce to the public the songwriting of a young Gordon Lightfoot, who was later to record its title song himself. The lyrics of the Gzowski–Tyson collaboration were a depiction of English-speaking Canadians speaking to French-speaking Canadians, through such lines as "How come we can't talk to each other anymore? / Why can't you see I'm changing, too?" The song represented an effort, as Tyson stated in the notes on the album's jacket, to "bridge the widening gap between the two peoples." Gzowski's last article in *Maclean's* appeared on October 17, 1964, and was entitled, "An Open Letter to the French Canadian Nationalists." In it, Gzowski mused on possible solutions to the "widening gap."

In the same way Gzowski would later find career opportunities in broadcasting in an expanding CBC, he encountered little resistance to his career advances in print journalism in the 1950s and 1960s. The jobs to be taken in a media career at the time were increasingly prestigious and lucrative, especially for men. In the 1950s, women were not barred from working in the media, but their career paths were steeper. Gzowski was appointed assistant editor at *Maclean's* in 1958, replacing Christina McCall. McCall is today a respected and successful journalist and author, who has gone on to write best-selling books about the Liberals in Canada (*Grits*) and, with her husband, Stephen Clarkson, about Prime Minister Trudeau (*Trudeau and Our Times*). While she had made $4,800 a year at the job at *Maclean's* (her title, with apparently similar duties, was "editorial assistant"), Gzowski's starting salary was $7,200, fifty per cent higher. No men were admitted to the lower category of "editorial assistant," but a half-dozen or so women were.

During his six years at *Maclean's*, Gzowski served as assistant editor, Preview editor (a department in the magazine, which featured short items about trends in society), Quebec editor, and managing editor. After resigning, he celebrated the event with champagne, in company with his co-workers, who at the time included Robert Fulford, a colleague who was to become a lifelong friend (figure 11). Gzowski was to return to *Maclean's* as editor for nine months in 1969–70.

What did an editor at *Maclean's* do in those days? According to Fulford, the duties were not as painstaking and intellectually rigorous as one might assume:

[I]n many cases editors find themselves publishing the least bad material available on the day the final list of contents is made up. Sometimes, when an editor is asked why this or that article was published, the only honest answer is, "It was all I had." (142)

Gzowski combined writing and editing during most of his years at *Maclean's*, and this meant that he gained experience in communicating with readers and also in mediating the flow of communication between owner and reader. So he has long had a practical sense not only for how to write for the readership of a magazine but also for how to establish its overall style and direction. Today, he keeps strong opinions on the role and mandate of the CBC, referring cynically to the "bean-counters" (those who measure and analyse market share, for example) at the Corporation.

Maclean's remains a parallel medium to that of *Morningside*. It is a précis of "current affairs" in Canada, prepared in a style that an audience will find accessible and stylistically coherent. Gzowski himself confirms the connection when he talks about his years at the magazine: "What I learned back then is the basis of the style I aspire to at *Morningside*" (Abley 24). As a result of this continuing interest, one of the first interviews he carried out during the 1993–94 season was with Robert Lewis, the editor of *Maclean's* magazine. Lewis had been editor since April 1993 and was hired to increase the readership and profitability of the magazine. During the interview, Gzowski seemed particularly concerned that the magazine should increase its "Canadian content," that the news it covers should generally be Canadian news, allowing the larger news magazines, such as *Time* and *Newsweek*, to cover international news.

A LASTING LOVE

As a former writer and editor at *Maclean's*, Gzowski has a kind of lifelong personal investment in its well-being and success. When he resigned from the magazine, over a matter of principle involving a story approved by the editor but not by the owners, Gzowski wrote that he thought the magazine had a special place in Canadian culture and that it compared favourably with competing American publications of the time ("The Time the Schick Hit the Fan" 150–51). Through writing for and championing a periodical that he considered better than its American counterparts, he seemed to be trying to "check the territorial ambitions of the United States," in the same way that his great-great-grandfather had:

> Canada has been very lucky about *Maclean's*, really. In recent years its English-language circulation has been held fairly deliberately around 550,000. In our English-language population of, say, 14 million that's equivalent to the 7 million sold in the U.S. by *Life*, *Look* or the *Saturday Evening Post*. Can anyone imagine one of those three magazines with a regular column by the equivalent of Robert Fulford? . . . There may be an awful lot of better magazines than *Maclean's* in the world, but there aren't many tougher, or more honest, *general* ones, and I think Canada has been a better place to live because of the guts *Maclean's* has shown.

Gzowski and his colleagues were not the only ones to make this kind of a congratulatory assessment of the magazine. Edmund Wilson, the American literary critic, had publicly complimented the *Maclean's* editors and writers of that era:

> Mr. Gzowski and his associates succeeded in transforming *Maclean's* from a rather inferior version of the kind of thing that we get in *McCall's* or the *Saturday Evening Post* into an outstanding journalistic achievement, an enterprising and intelligent coverage — the fiction department having been dropped — of all phases of Canadian life, by what I suppose must have been one of the ablest staffs ever got together in Canada. It is regrettable that a change of management which involved putting a curb on the free expression of the findings and views of these writers should have resulted in the resignation of almost the whole staff and converted the magazine back again from a serious venture in reporting to an exploit in the higher pulp. (4)

Gzowski's work at *Maclean's* from 1958 to 1964 represents a period in which the young writer took a plainly idealistic

FIGURE 15

Jarvis Street studios of the CBC *in Toronto, Gzowski's base for*
Morningside *for more than a decade. This photo was taken in June*
1992, just before the consolidation of all CBC *staff in the Corporation's*
new Broadcast Centre, a "smoke-free" facility, in downtown Toronto.
PHOTO COURTESY THE CBC

approach to his work. His professed principles of journalism were, by his own statements, uncompromising. In fact, the reason for his resignation from the magazine had been doubly entwined with those principles. He quit because he could not accept that a vice-president of Maclean-Hunter could "kill" a story over the wishes of the editor, Ken Lefolii. For the writers and editors at the magazine, such a decision represented an affront to their intellectual independence. Moreover, the content itself of the dead story was connected to the journalistic sensibility. Harry Bruce had written a story about a strike by the International Typographical Union at Toronto's newspapers. Maclean-Hunter vice-president Ron McEachern said the story was "unfair to both sides." The story was not published. Lefolii resigned, and Gzowski, along with four other writers, followed suit.

Gzowski seemed to believe that the magazine represented something intangibly delicate and pure in the midst of a sordid world of commercialism. Yet this view was contradictory. The appointment of Lefolii as editor was a sign, according to Gzowski, that Maclean-Hunter, the publishing company that owned the magazine, was both courageous and cowardly. It had bravely appointed the editor, Ken Lefolii, giving him "control of their most important property." But then it "began taking the cutting edge off Lefolii's editorial control" ("The Time the Schick Hit the Fan" 151).

Similarly, Gzowski said that, inspired by the magazine's innovation and editorial boldness, he "worked harder there than I ever hope to work at anything again" (151). He suggested that the trail-blazing work of the magazine's writers and editors had been instilled by a succession of editors, beginning with Arthur Irwin from 1945 to 1950, then continuing with Ralph Allen during the 1950s and Blair Fraser in 1960 and 1961, and culminating with the work of Gzowski's boss, Ken Lefolii. In fact, Gzowski estimated that during those years, the editorial drive for quality had had a direct financially quantifiable result at the magazine — almost $9 million worth of lawsuits against it.

Yet the magazine did not have a higher wall between editorial and advertising content than any other commercial magazine — before, during, or after Gzowski's tenure. Christina McCall was writing (albeit in 1958, some years before this celebration of editorial principle) about "The Brave New World of Trailer Living" in anticipation of ad copy to come. The magazine would publish, adjacent to its masthead in one of its 1961 issues, such fearless claims as the following, paid for by the pulp and paper industry of Canada: "Through research, the pulp and paper companies are increasing the value of the woodlands, thereby providing greater benefits and great prosperity for Canadians everywhere." Such self-promotion by advertisers was not unusual at the time for a privately owned medium.

Maclean's was no less calculating than any other periodical in its willingness to allow the "news hole," as some have called it, to provide occasional ironic contrasts with the claims of advertisers. But Gzowski had a refreshing naïvety about the extent to which he personally remained completely on one side of the line that distinguished the writer/editor from the advertiser/owner. By resigning on a matter of "editorial principle," Gzowski maintained for himself a personal mythology of himself as a competitive, self-contained actor who was quite immune to the contaminations of commercial, political, or even personal pressure.

In support of this view of himself, he would tell and retell the story of how he had exposed the facts behind an advertising campaign to promote Schick razor blades. As managing editor of *Maclean's*, he had written that "sixteen Toronto Maple Leaf hockey players had each been paid $50 without even all having to shave with one blade" ("The Time the Schick Hit the Fan" 150). In fact, this anecdote provided the introduction, which appeared in *Canadian Forum* magazine, to his public explanation of why he had resigned from *Maclean's*. It prepared the reader for the thesis that journalistic principles were something Gzowski would guard at all costs.

It all seems so innocent now: the young writer quitting because he is persuaded that his employers do not share his disinterested and publicly minded view of the world.

But Gzowski did not spend much time mourning his fate. He took the job of editor of the *Star Weekly* in 1967. In 1968, it went out of business. As a result, he lost a salary of $35,000 a year, a large income for the time. The bad times followed the good times with a rhythmic inevitability during Gzowski's years as a journalist.

Romantically, he ended his career as a print journalist — except for the brief interval as editor of *Maclean's* — by sailing to England with his family on the *Aleksandr Pushkin* for a holiday. The Gzowskis spent eight days on the ship, travelling from Montreal to London. Gzowski remembers the vacation as confirming the impressions he already held about the cultures he was to observe. On the ship, the Russians dutifully acted with formality; they conformed to the popular image of them as chess players:

> A Russian would no more think of making a spontaneous gesture of friendliness — or enmity — than he would of moving his rook along a diagonal. I say this, mind you, from my vast experience of eight days on their proud and efficient ship. But that is precisely my point. Everything — *everything* — fit what I already knew. ("The Global Village" 35)

The trip had a comforting effect on Gzowski. It was not the kind of disorienting, creative disruption that some of his contemporaries were seeking in travel. Rather, it made him more content to be in Canada and to redouble his efforts at trying to define and reinforce a notion of the Canadian identity. "It was a wonderful time," he has said of the 1960s (*Morningside*, November 18, 1992). Having a birthday in 1934, he mused, had kept him and others born during that time out of all wars. In addition, "It made us just the right age during the 60s. That was a good time in life." His vacation abroad was short, for Gzowski was soon back in Canada trying his hand at a medium that he had known intimately as a boy but was to exploit now for the first time in his career: radio.

FIGURE 16

Peter in 1970.

PHOTO COURTESY THE CBC,
ROBERT C. RAGSDALE PHOTOGRAPHY

3. Experiments in Journalism

NATIONALISM AND THE CBC

In 1969, Gzowski spent some months hosting a show called *Radio Free Friday*, but that was interrupted late that year by his appointment as editor of *Maclean's*. As the person responsible for setting the editorial direction of the magazine until his name disappeared from the masthead in August 1970, Gzowski was sympathetic to some of the leanings of those Canadians who were living in what would become known as the "counterculture." As editor of *Maclean's*, for example, he commissioned Bob Bossin, a self-proclaimed "token radical," to write a column every three months about current social issues. These pieces were often strongly critical of Canadian institutions and decision-makers. Gzowski did not take an iconoclastic approach to journalism, but according to Bossin, he gave those who did, like Bossin, "free reign" (Bossin, "Interview," 1993 [Adria]). Gzowski carried this sympathetic approach from journalism to radio, attempting in each show with which he was associated to bring about some change in style, content, or presentation.

In 1971, Gzowski began working on his first extended project on CBC Radio — a new and innovative program called *This Country in the Morning*, which replaced a morning show called *Gerussi*. *This Country* was a three-hour show broadcast each weekday morning featuring interviews, recipes, music, skits, and essays. In short, it was a precursor to *Morningside*, although the earlier show had a more flexible structure. As Gzowski describes it, he and the show's executive producer, Alex Frame, would "pick up a file of letters and scribbled notes, and we'd amble down to the studio" (*The Private Voice* 198). For many in the audience, the show seemed to meet a national need. In fact,

FIGURE 17

This Country in the Morning *(1972)*.
[Alex Frame is pictured above, bottom, on the right.]
PHOTOS COURTESY OF JOHN REEVES

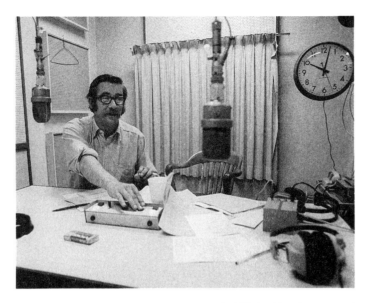

according to Gzowski, people sometimes asked him if he and Frame were trying "to keep the country together." That question is not a specious one, given the unique mandate of the CBC and its subsidiary, CBC Radio. The CBC allowed Gzowski an opportunity to contribute to the Corporation's mandate, which called for a distinctly Canadian broadcasting service, while simultaneously working to resolve some of the contradictions of his personal history.

Like the British Broadcasting Corporation on which it was loosely modelled, the Canadian Broadcasting Corporation is funded by government, which spends about a billion dollars a year on it. (CBC Radio, which first went on the air in 1936, is not required to generate revenues through advertising.) Because of this special status, the CBC, including CBC Radio, has a legislated duty to fulfil a public mandate. The question of *This Country's* role in national unity was directly tied to that mandate. The mandate stated that the national broadcasting service should:

(i) be a balanced service of information, enlightenment and entertainment for people of different ages, interests and tastes covering the whole range of programming in fair proportion,

(ii) be extended to all parts of Canada, as public funds become available,

(iii) be in English and French, serving the special needs of geographic regions, and actively contributing to the flow and exchange of cultural and regional information and entertainment, and

(iv) contribute to the development of national unity and provide for a continuing expression of Canadian identity. (Bird 590)

Thus, Gzowski's work in CBC Radio has meant that his role has by definition included the exhortation to contribute to national unity. Gzowski has embraced that role with vigour. When, as is made clear in the citations for his honorary degrees, Gzowski is recognized as having contributed to a sense of the Canadian identity, it is in part because he has associated himself with an institution whose mandate has expressly called for such a contribution.

This connection between nationalism and the role of the CBC is one Gzowski commented on when he was interviewed for the publicity accompanying the National Film Board documentary entitled *Family: A Loving Look at CBC Radio*:

> One of the reasons I've always thought that CBC Radio works so well in Canada is that there are no models for us; there's no American model. We don't do good sitcoms; we're not good stand-up comics. But there are a lot of things we do extraordinarily well. And where we can have our own wry sense of humour and our own ability to document things, we're great documentarists. That's what CBC Radio does.

When he accepted his honorary Doctor of Letters from Queen's University in 1990, he suggested that such honours were not for him personally but for CBC Radio. That day, this "godfather of Confederation," as he was introduced, also stated very clearly the relationship he feels he has with his audience. Canadians, he said, could remain united:

> However profound our differences, our similarities outnumber them: our gentleness, our essential politesse . . . , our history, our institutions, our "melting pot," our parliamentary system, our sense of the land, our understanding that in a harsh, underpopulated landscape, people have to huddle together against the cold. ("Convocation")

Similarly, when introducing an anecdote about interviewing Simon Reisman, the chief Canadian negotiator for the Canada–U.S. free trade agreement, Gzowski devoted several pages of *The Private Voice* to defending Canadian efforts to building another version of life as it is lived in North America. Efforts that resulted

FIGURE 18

Morningside *letters* — *Peter and Shelagh Rodgers (1990)*.
PHOTO COURTESY THE CBC, GEORGE KRAYCHYK PHOTOGRAPHY

in a national railway, an airline, banks, and a public broadcasting system.

Murray McLauchlan has mentioned Gzowski's efforts to promote nationalism when he has spoken about the broadcaster's calls during the mid-1980s for a renewal in the career of Stompin' Tom Connors. According to McLauchlan, Gzowski's search for a quintessential Canadian quality or characteristic is itself a hallmark of Gzowski's career:

> Peter Gzowski has made Stompin' Tom Connors into a symbol of all Canadians who have been so vilified and laughed at by the media that they decided to quit . . . Peter has a sort of romantic view of what Stompin' Tom is, what he does, and what he represents. Peter is looking for a great Canadian "issue." He is a curious man. He is a refined character, in the style of Gordon Sinclair or Pierre Berton. He has a very specific point of view, and he searches for "Canadian-ness" in out-of-the-way places and out-of-the-way people. (Adria 41)

Gzowski has become Canada's best-loved broadcaster by attaching his personal aspirations to those of a collectivity. In doing so, his work echoes the words of George Grant, Canada's only pious nationalist, who said that Canada's secret strength was the subordination of the individual to the collective. Gzowski's life and work have been considered exemplary by many Canadians — this is made clear by the honorary degrees and other tributes he has received — but especially by those who are persuaded by the arguments of Canadian nationalists.

THE CANADIAN NATIONALISTS MEET

Gzowski's career was nurtured by a period of cultural growth in Canada in the 1960s and 1970s. The political and economic muscle required for a real expansion in the cultural infrastructure of the country was at hand. The unique admixture of Gzowski's personality, nationalism, and the CBC was to prove attractive to one particular Canadian nationalist, who wanted to translate Gzowski's radio show into print.

In 1974, Gzowski compiled his first book, *Peter Gzowski's Book About This Country in the Morning*. Its genesis was rooted in the twin themes of nationalism and the tension between the broadcast and printed word. Mel Hurtig, the Edmonton publisher, heard *This Country in the Morning* and thought a book based on the show — or any book associated with *This Country* — would prove popular. Within hours after a book was reviewed or discussed on the program, inquiries about it would flood his Edmonton shops. (Hurtig was at the time a bookseller as well as a publisher.) When the book in question was a Hurtig book, his publishing company would note an increase in demand for the book from booksellers across the country.

Hurtig could see in Gzowski's success on radio the articulation of a nationalist vision. He has said that *This Country*, as well as its protégé, *Morningside*, connected the geographical pockets of Canada. Later, he was to liken the unifying function of both programs to that of the Canadian Pacific Railway (Hurtig, "Interview," 1992 [Adria]). *Peter Gzowski's Book About This Country in the Morning* put into printed form the quirky, eclectic, nationalistic flavour of the radio program.

The meeting of the two men was to be followed by a parting of ways for the nationalist movement in Canada. Hurtig and Gzowski were to follow different paths in advocating a more autonomous Canadian state. Hurtig had been building his publishing house at the same time as he had begun consolidating a political platform. He had run for the Trudeau Liberals against Marcel Lambert in Edmonton West in 1972. He lost and the next year quit politics. Twenty years later, of course, he took a renewed interest in politics, forming the National Party, whose policies would include cancelling the North American Free Trade Agreement and enacting legislation that would reduce foreign ownership in the country. Hurtig was to continue the path of a directly political approach to promoting national independence.

He wanted to promote in Canada a "national interest," which would be expressed by a series of policies by which Canadian ownership and control of resources and economic activity would be ensured. For Gzowski, the efforts on behalf of national independence have been just as intense, but the route taken has been more indirect. Through his writing and broadcasting, Gzowski has advocated an overt expression of a shared set of national values: the values of a peaceable, vaguely British, conciliatory nation. He wanted to promote a debate, not so much about the national interest, but about the national identity.

For Hurtig, nationalism is a political pursuit; for Gzowski it is a cultural one. While Gzowski on radio might frequently refer to his values in this regard, it would be difficult to refer to them in the political sense that Hurtig has done. Gzowski's version of nationalism is one that can be discussed openly on a publicly owned radio broadcast such as *This Country*, while Hurtig's cannot. If Gzowski was in sympathy with the objectives of the National Party during the 1993 federal election, he could not, of course, articulate those sympathies publicly. But he could continue to call for more Canadian content in cultural activities, such as the arts, broadcasting, even sports.

I have already suggested that radio was a means for Gzowski of resolving the dissonance he perceived between the aural (that is, the American cultural production he heard on radio) and the visual (both the symbols of daily life in Galt and his family heritage, especially the large public works erected by Sir Casimir) and that his interest in things literary was connected to his "romantic traditional" sensibility. Books provided another means by which Gzowski could try to resolve the clash of the aural and the visual, since a book constituted visual evidence of the aural articulation of Canadian radio. For a radio program to gain the status of a statement of national unity, it would have to be translated into print. We can consider the matter of Gzowski's interest in the broadcast and printed word in terms again of the *figure* and *ground* metaphor of painting. First, through radio Gzowski synthesized cultural noise, a *figure* against the *ground* of America. Then, through publication he added to the written (and therefore, "legitimate") visual record of Canada, thereby enhancing the *ground* of Canadian culture.

The days of *This Country* were heady. Gzowski felt that he had found a place for himself, socially and professionally. His interviews with Pierre Trudeau and John Diefenbaker were considered important achievements by many journalists. His career, it seemed, was hitting its stride. In the introduction to the *This Country* book he acknowledged that fact when he thanked the people who had worked with him on the program:

> [T]o those behind the microphone and in front of the radio, I owe debts I can never repay for the most rewarding years of my life. (9)

When asked why *This Country* came to an end after three successful years, he says,

> There was no doubt I was tired . . . At the end of three years it just felt like we'd done it. And I just didn't think I could put the "harness" on again in the fall. Also, we had already begun to talk about taking [the show] to television, which was tempting, seductive. And there was no pattern for anything. *This Country in the Morning* was brand new. It had evolved from an acorn into what it had become. It was very satisfying for me. Given everything I know now, I would never have left it at that time. ("Interview," 1992 [Adria])

Personally, however, the severed connections to his parents were still raw and his marriage was about to come apart. The professional focus for this critical period was a television program he was to host called *90 Minutes Live*.

90 MINUTES LIVE

While he was hosting a CBC Stereo program entitled *Gzowski on FM*, Gzowski and his *This Country* producer, Alex Frame, had discussed the possibility of creating a television show that would have the same aspirations as their efforts on radio. At an expanding CBC, the idea caught the imagination of the executives, especially after Gzowski and Frame began collaborating with Peter Hernndorf, the Corporation's head of public affairs. The show ran for two seasons and was cancelled in 1976. It was a "talk show" modelled, whether the creators admitted it or not, on similar programs such as *The Tonight Show*. Following the mandate and culture at the CBC, the guests on the show were almost invariably Canadians; Margaret Atwood, Pierre Berton, David Suzuki, Ken Dryden, and Patrick Watson all appeared. Others appeared, as well: author Kurt Vonnegut, Jr., *Penthouse* publisher Bob Guccione, and counter-culture figure Timothy Leary. The show featured poets, politicians, comedians, and musicians. But it didn't have the excitement of its competitors. Perhaps the producers were too wary of controversy. Bob Bossin, who completed a pilot version of the program, was not invited to appear on air, because he had verbally attacked John Bassett, a Toronto media magnate, during the pilot ("Interview," Bossin, 1993 [Adria]). If decisions about which guests to invite onto the show were made using such a criterion, as Bossin suggests, the show might have been too much under the sway of what Gzowski has called the "bean-counters." Officially, the reason the show was cancelled was that the number of viewers, as determined by survey, was too small.

I detect a change in Gzowski's journalistic approach between *90 Minutes Live* and *Morningside*, which may help to explain, apart from the ratings, the show's demise. The change is connected to the difference that Marshall McLuhan identifies between the characteristics of a "hot" medium, such as radio, and a "cool" one, such as television. (According to McLuhan, radio is hot because only one sense is used for apprehending it and because the actual broadcast signals are highly defined.) On television, Gzowski seemed to sense that his "definition" was not sharp enough. He showed an edge to his audience, which some watchers found cut too deeply. On radio, on the other hand, Gzowski is much less in "focus." He stammers, changes the pitch of his voice, and lets others do the talking. In McLuhan's terms, the audience must work harder to complete Gzowski's radio "image." On television, no involvement of the audience was required and none, it seems, was offered.

The problems Gzowski encountered on *90 Minutes Live* were, some were to assume, chronic, for in 1985, Gzowski was to make another short-lived attempt at television, with a program called *Gzowski & Co.* (the title a play on the name of a firm established by Sir Casimir). The show featured him travelling across the country doing interviews with famous and not-so-famous Canadians. It was cancelled in 1987, a victim partly of general budget cutbacks at the CBC that year, which also saw the cancellation of the popular children's show *Fraggle Rock* and a scaling down of the nightly current affairs show *The Journal*.

Interestingly, *90 Minutes Live* and *Gzowski & Co*, as relatively unsuccessful as they were in the eyes of CBC analysts and decision-makers, were not Gzowski's only attempts to develop a role as a television host. In September 1964, Gzowski auditioned to become the co-host of *This Hour Has Seven Days*. The show was to become, with Patrick Watson and Laurier LaPierre as hosts, one of Canada's most influential public affairs programs. But after trying out at the CBC television studio just down the street from where he would begin his work two decades later as host of *Morningside*, Gzowski was turned down for the job at *This Hour*. Among the others competing to work on the show that autumn was Peter Jennings, now of ABC network fame.

The events of the years immediately following the cancellation of *90 Minutes Live* would further inflame Gzowski's personal and professional wounds. The mid-1970s constituted a time of personal crisis and introspection for him. During this period he ended his marriage, which had lasted for two decades. Since 1971, the family had lived in North Toronto, at 98 Lytton Boulevard (figure 12), spending summers at Ward's Island. After his separation, Gzowski would live apart from his family, visiting his children when he could. He now regularly visits his children and

FIGURE 19

90 Minutes Live.
PHOTO COURTESY THE CBC

FIGURE 20

Halifax town crier Peter Cox, Gzowski, and John Candy (1979).
PHOTO COURTESY THE CBC

grandchildren, often recounting the experiences in the column he writes for *Canadian Living* magazine.

In 1978, Gzowski's natural father died, a death, Gzowski would say, which had been hastened by "booze and purposelessness" (Abley 26). The severance from his natural parents was now complete, and it came at a time when his professional life was coming apart. Although the three years after the show ended were busy and productive — he published a book in each of the years 1979, 1980, and 1981 — it was also a time for reconsidering the direction of his personal life and career. Stung by the critics, he retreated to Rockwood, Ontario, a small town near Guelph — and, significantly, not far from Galt. There, he seemed to find some peace. He worked on two books: *Spring Tonic*, then *The Sacrament*.

BACK TO THE SMALL TOWN

Gzowski has described Rockwood as "achingly pretty." It was a community in which his neighbours knew what he was up to. They called Gzowski's house, which had been a restaurant owned by two young men, "Ian and Sylvia's place." The landscape was similar to the one he had known in Galt. When Gzowski was surrounded by the geographical features and social customs of his boyhood, a change in his sensibility emerged. The intimate bonds of the small town became tangible again, and Gzowski's public personality began to reflect the fact. Moving to Rockwood was an influence on the evolution of his approach to media. In Rockwood, he became reconnected to the values of the small town, which, thereafter, were to become more evident in his work as a broadcaster.

Gzowski had spent twenty years away from the small town of his childhood. Now he returned to a small town to find comfort by reconsidering the values that he had assimilated early in life. The values that he had simply breathed in as a child, Gzowski now tried to apply like a salve. In Galt he had spent time letting

FIGURE 21

Peter in 1976.
PHOTO COURTESY THE CBC

the wounds of a broken family heal; he allowed the same process to begin in Rockwood. Galt had taught him the sensibilities of civility and politesse, both of which had been rubbed raw in the events of the past few years. In Rockwood he tried to decide whether those values could be enlivened in his professional life. In Galt he had learned the value of social cohesion through observing the interlinked activities of business and community. During his hiatus in Rockwood he reconsidered the wisdom of encouraging, as he had done at *Maclean's*, the acerbic wit of someone like Bob Bossin, which was directed at corporate owners and members of the political élite. Perhaps that was not what was really needed to give strength to an autonomous Canadian identity.

As he had done when he was sick as a child, the emotionally vulnerable Gzowski in Rockwood, alone now most of the day, tuned in to the receiver:

> Living in Rockwood . . . I listened to the radio as I seldom had before. And I learned much about what Don Harron [the host of *Morningside* at the time] was doing wrong and probably about what I had done wrong, and generally what the CBC had done wrong. I began to think that should I ever get back to radio, I would never do *that* again, or try not to. ("Interview," 1992 [Adria])

The *new* Gzowski — the one after *90 Minutes Live* — was not hiding something from his listeners, but he was more aware of the particular social, and even political, power he held. This realization evoked a reticence. He was to hestitate before forming questions and responses. He waited. The change showed in his public expressions. While on *90 Minutes Live*, for example, Gzowski might — in fact did — mention to Bob Guccione (the ebullient publisher of *Penthouse*) that he, Gzowski, was a faithful reader of the magazine, the host of *Morningside* would have asked, instead, thoughtful questions about the role of pornography in Canadian society. (In any case, as Gzowski told me in 1992, Guccione would never and could never be invited to

Morningside.) This is not to say that Gzowski became less frank during his sabbatical, only that his notion of how one maintains the delicate bonds of civic coalescence had changed.

When he decided to take on the host's job at *Morningside*, Gzowski had become a different man from the host of *90 Minutes Live*. He had spent three years considering his career. Even his appearance was more substantial. He was heavier, and bearded. The image he conveyed on radio was gentler; the experience of the past three years had, paradoxically, toughened him but left him more emotionally vulnerable. Before 1979, his career advance had been without the impediment of failure, but now he knew the pain of personal and professional failure. After twice losing his family, once as son and once as father, and after trying to mend those severed connections through work, Gzowski's nerves were closer to the skin. In a quotation from *The Private Voice* referring to media criticism of *90 Minutes Live*, this change reveals itself: "The critics *weren't* writing about my "work"; they were writing about *me*" (173–74). The new-found awareness of his vulnerability was to become apparent to his audience and to his guests when he again became a broadcaster. If there was one thing listeners could name in trying to explain Gzowski's powers as an interviewer, it was the identification he established with his audience. Whereas in *90 Minutes Live* Gzowski used the mask of "public persona," after the end of that show he used that of the participant-observer. He understood from experience, better than he had before, the particulars of emotional distress.

SPRINGTIME OF THE SOUL

Part of the process of reconnection in Rockwood took place as he put together *Spring Tonic*, published in 1979. The format of the book is much like that of its predecessor, *Peter Gzowski's Book About This Country in the Morning*. However, the theme of *Spring Tonic* is not, as it is in This Country and the five *Morningside* books, a radio show. Rather, it is the set of rituals associated with the end of winter in Canada and the beginning of spring.

The rebirth to be celebrated in *Spring Tonic*, Gzowski points out in his introduction, is both literal and figurative. Many of the poems, stories, and interviews in the book are indeed associated with the season during which the street-cleaning machines appear after a period of hibernation and the procreative urge is everywhere to be inferred. But the other kind of spring, the other rebirth to which the book is devoted, is personal and professional. Gzowski's marriage had ended and he had failed to accomplish, for the first time, an important goal in his career, in this case success as a television host.

There is a springtime of the soul, Gzowski writes, which is as important as the season associated with a particular inclination of the earth as it revolves around the sun:

> I started the book because of my own need to dream, and because I felt that need begin to be filled. . . . I wanted the therapy of helping to shape something that would make me feel good not only because it was fun to do but because the result of that work would make some other people feel good as well. (10)

Spring Tonic was the second and last book by Gzowski to be released by Hurtig, who was to garner national acclaim six years later for his publication of the *Canadian Encyclopedia*. By publishing *Spring Tonic*, Hurtig lost, by his report, $35,000. A few years earlier, he had also lost his editor-in-chief, Jan Walter, who left Edmonton for Toronto, moving in with Gzowski in Rockwood. For *The Sacrament* and all his books since, Gzowski has dealt with McClelland and Stewart. He was left out of the first edition of the *Encyclopedia*.

ANOTHER REBIRTH

The motif of spring, of a rebirth, would figure again in Gzowski's journalistic prose only a year after the release of

Spring Tonic. The narrative of *The Sacrament*, a book of reportage, juxtaposes the creeping warmth of spring in the White Cloud Mountains of Idaho against the stark necessities of the human body. A young man and a young woman survive a plane crash, as two other passengers — the woman's father and the pilot — do not. The man is married to the woman's sister. The two have no particular religious beliefs, but they find emotional and seemingly physical strength in such elemental activities as singing hymns and holding a simple funeral service for the father. They find meaning in the fact that in the hours following the crash, in which all the passengers fall in and out of consciousness, the father, just before dying, has given his daughter his coat. After some days without sustenance, the survivors become convinced that their deliverance can only come of eating the dead body, which they do.

The author of *The Sacrament* is made a character in the action, albeit a reticent one. Gzowski abandons the role of spectator — the "reporter," the one who records — and takes on that of the participant-observer. The participant-observer has a bias. He expresses sympathy for the two survivors, although he reveals his position only through implication:

> Self-conscious visitors will sometimes find themselves groping for euphemisms for cannibalism, or trying to avoid figures of speech that may seem to have unfortunate ramifications. (199)

The "self-conscious visitors" include, of course, and even exclusively, Gzowski himself. We know this, but we are made to abide by the conventions of reportage and ignore it. (Then, perhaps the subtle modification of the identity of the intruder was simply an editing convention.) Likewise, in the acknowledgements section at the end of the book, Gzowski refers to the actors' home town — Estevan in southern Saskatchewan, not far from Moose Jaw — as "a part of the world I first knew as a newspaperman twenty years ago." The stance, that of the participant-observer, is the one we recognize from *Morningside*. We know Gzowski's sympathies and biases, but these are *implied* in the interviews he does, and he is careful to subordinate them to the mood of the interview.

As with *Spring Tonic*, the personal meaning in *The Sacrament* to be gleaned for the participants in the drama is clear enough. We may be delivered from untimely death, but also, one infers, from alcoholism, boredom, laziness, addiction. The incident leaves the actors, and Gzowski himself, we presume, changed somehow, and for the better. The corporate meaning, on the other hand, is connected to the human need for ritual and myth.

Gzowski ends *The Sacrament* with the account of an incident fraught with meaning. Brent Dyer, one of the crash survivors, honours the vow he made on the mountainside to love his wife more deeply after they are reunited. For her part, his wife symbolically returns to her father the "gift" he had given to her sister and husband:

> In June of 1979, in a quiet ceremony at St. John the Baptist Church, Brent and Cindy Dyer were remarried in the Catholic faith. After the ceremony, Cindy laid her bridal bouquet of lilacs on her father's grave. (201)

Rekindled love and the implied restatement of the motif of a father giving a precious gift to his children: the mythical implications of the story are clearest in this passage. That it was written at a time when Gzowski's own roles as father and son were in transition — his father had recently died and his marriage just ended — gives it the weight of implied autobiography.

A thematic ending such as this one is uncharacteristic of the "inverted pyramid" news story that Gzowski had learned to write for the Timmins *Daily Press* some twenty-five years previous. In that literary form, and to allow for an editor to cut "from the bottom up," the details of an incident become increasingly dispensable with each succeeding paragraph. *The Sacrament* reveals the aspirations of the New Journalists, whose work was

FIGURE 22

Peter in 1979.
PHOTO COURTESY THE CBC

typified by the techniques of the Americans Norman Mailer and Tom Wolfe. The New Journalists interpreted current events through the filter of their own senses and experience. Rejecting the "invisible," anonymous journalist of the past, they combined the techniques of fiction with those of non-fiction. It is an influence Gzowski has discussed in *The Private Voice*. *The Sacrament* is characterized by a dramatic structure, dialogue, and technical explanations of such phenomena as *transubstantiation* (a religious term referring to the sacrament of communion but connoting the consumption of human flesh) and *jargon aphasia* (the neurological condition of the plane's pilot, which resulted from an injury sustained in the crash).

The book deals with a sensitive subject: cannibalism, as it is baldly stated in library indexes. About this topic and others, Gzowski is delicate but frank, relying on the craft of journalism to suggest in literary terms what, in practical terms, is unimaginable. He leads up to the moment by using a term such as *silent communion* (40). He uses phrases that include, "he [Don, the woman's father] gave his life for you" (46), and "Don had given 'the kid' one last present" (37). The book has a tight structure, which is a foil to Gzowski's usually meandering prose. He gets underneath the journalist's story to the mythical relationships that inform it. *The Sacrament* presents Gzowski at his journalistic best.

HOCKEY AND HORSES

The year he began hosting *Morningside*, Gzowski published *The Game of Our Lives*. Wayne Gretzky suggested the idea of a book on the Edmonton Oilers, and Gzowski travelled with the team during the 1980–81 hockey season and wrote about the experience. The manuscript was read by Gary Ross, a writer and editor with *Saturday Night* magazine, who was to write an award-winning book of non-fiction entitled *Stung*, which seems to have been influenced by some of the journalistic techniques Gzowski used in *The Sacrament*. Twenty-five thousand copies of *The Game of Our Lives* were printed — with seven thousand of these mailed as gifts to Oilers season-ticket holders of 1981–82 — and the book became a best seller.

There was in Gzowski's sports writing the same tension between the point-counterpoint of American and Canadian culture that had been evident in his approach to radio and newspapers. The American influence was pervasive and powerful, but it was not to be regarded as cause for resignation. Similar to the inspiration of the Algonquin Round Table (a small group of New Yorkers writing in the 1930s and 1940s) for his magazine writing, the models for Gzowski's sports journalism were to be found south of the border, as he stated in *The Private Voice*:

> I had thought for a long time that the kind of serious writing Americans had enjoyed on baseball might be matched on our national sport, and, having loved playing hockey as a kid and written about its heroes for magazines, I thought I might give it a try. (205)

The following year Gzowski released *An Unbroken Line*, a book whose theme is the parallel between the family lines of the Ontario élite and those of Canadian thoroughbreds. It's a book characterized by the kind of unexplained contradiction to be heard on *Morningside*: the pacing of the presentation is used to cover inconsistencies in the content. Gzowski himself has become ambivalent on the book's status in his writing portfolio, as he told *Saturday Night* magazine: "It may be my best book . . . or my worst. I don't know" (Abley 27). The argument that Gzowski adopted the role of participant-observer while writing *The Sacrament* could be applied in inversion to the failure of *An Unbroken Line*. In the later book, Gzowski is again in the mode of "public persona," the stance of the host of *90 Minutes Live*. The empathy and reticence of the participant-observer's stance, Gzowski's strength as an interviewer, never take a firm hold. In spite of this failing, I found in the course of my research that a cloth edition of the book had been duly placed in the Veterinary Medical Library of the University of Saskatchewan, an indication that many readers simply didn't know what to do with the book. After *An Unbroken Line* appeared, it would be six years until, with the publication of *The Private Voice* in 1988, he would release any book other than one of the volumes of the *Morningside Papers*.

4. Morningside

On the cover of its November 1986 edition, *Saturday Night* magazine named Peter Gzowski "the voice of Canada." He is one of only a few radio journalists in Canada whose face, as well as his voice, is widely recognized. His popularity is based mainly on his accomplishments as the host of *Morningside*. Gzowski has created a universe on *Morningside*. For three hours, every weekday morning, you can live somewhere in the ether, far from the place of the show's origination. Until its move to the new Broadcasting Centre in the business district of downtown Toronto, the show was produced for Gzowski's first ten years from an ancient building on Jarvis Street that formerly housed a girl's school (figure 15).

Morningside is a variety show, with regular panel discussions on business and politics. It features reports from each province and from the north. Occasionally Gzowski acts as a host for games or panels. On a single program, I heard a long interview with Annie Lennox (formerly of the rock band Eurythmics), a discussion on the scientific phenomenon of background radiation (with implications no less important than whether the "big bang" theory is still tenable), a "Report from Alberta," a letter from a gentleman residing in Elk Point in the same province, an item about gardening, another on the première of a national magazine, and yet another on a new Canadian movie. The show is eclectic and informal, with a stylized presentation and pacing.

The centrepiece of the show is the feature interviews. The interview subjects may be politicians, authors, musicians, entertainers. The conversations may be light-hearted or serious. Gzowski treats each guest differently. When Pierre Trudeau talked about the Meech Lake proposal in 1987, the interview itself became an event that was covered by all the national media. The compelling aspect of an interview with someone famous or powerful is that the subject is presented in an intimate setting, having a conversation with Gzowski, whom members of the audience see, in turn, as a surrogate for themselves. The result is a simulation of the personal and the individual in what is actually a media event for mass consumption. On the other hand, the interview may be as light as they come on radio: a chat, for example, with the pop singer Céline Dion or a feature on tying flies for fishing.

Many listeners wonder how it is that the relaxed, seamless flow that is a *Morningside* broadcast actually comes together. If it is true that the mood of the show is informal and seemingly improvisational in its production, the preparatory stages to that mood are, according to Gzowski, something else:

> *Morningside* is just a machine that devours stories and infor-
> mation and people and guests, just gobbles them up every
> day. And the producers themselves are on the phone inter-
> viewing, pre-interviewing the guests, finding the guests . . .
> (*Family*)

Features make it to air by a complex, fluid process of planning, discussion, negotiation, and preparation that involves Gzowski, the executive producer, a raft of producers, and, of course, the interview subjects and other sources. The central figures in the features' conception and development are the producers, most of whom are young, articulate, well-educated, and poorly paid media enthusiasts whose job it is to come up with ideas for the show and then to transform those ideas into features for broad-cast. The producers work long hours and receive drastically less glory than the "on-air personality." After the release of the first *Morningside* book, one of the producers expressed bitterness about this inequity: "It pissed me off. . . . The producers got no credit even for work *we* had commissioned" (Abley 27). Gzowski does publicly thank the producers for their work, especially through written acknowledgement in the *Morningside* books. After the comment by the disgruntled producer was made public, the acknowledgements have included the producers' names. Still, Gzowski has complained about having to deal with the turnover of staff and the resulting inexperience that has become an inevitable part of the show's production machine. When he was again considering leaving the CBC in 1991, a period documented in the NFB's *Family*, he identified the producers' inexperience as something that made him want to refuse to return to the show. He told Alex Frame, a former colleague from the days of *This Country in the Morning* but with whom he was now negotiating his contract: "I don't want to come limping back and be grumpy all the time and feel that I'm teaching journalism."

The process that results in the birth of a *Morningside* feature goes something like this. Staff meetings are held occasionally, attended by Gzowski, the producers, perhaps a CBC researcher to provide advice about ratings and public opinion, and the show's executive producer. The executive producer is Gzowski's boss, carrying out such managerial functions as formally asking him to observe the CBC's no-smoking policy, and receiving Gzowski's signed contract for services. Since Gzowski is one of the Corporation's highest paid staff members, earning an estimated $180,000 a year, the latter is no trivial task.

The first of the season's staff meetings is held in late summer, before the season actually starts in September, either at Gzowski's cottage on Lake Simcoe or at a hotel suite in the city. Throughout the season, regular weekly story meetings are held in the *Morningside* office. At the story meetings, the producers' plans are discussed, providing Gzowski and the executive producer an opportunity to guide or influence the balance of topics and guests. One year, for example, Gzowski felt more attention should be directed towards issues arising out of Quebec; there is a more or less constant gesture to try to improve the proportion of stories devoted to native and women's issues or other current concerns.

Based on the guidance they receive at the story meetings, the producers set out. A producer makes initial contact with guests and in many cases pre-interviews them by telephone. This is a screening process that sometimes results in a decision not to proceed with an on-air feature. The reason for such a decision often has to do with the subject's style and presentation. "Good radio" calls for thoughtful, articulate, expressive, and lively guests. Not all knowledgeable or even interesting potential guests have these characteristics. For the features that are to proceed to broadcast, the producer prepares the "greens," sheets on which are typed the introductions, notes, questions, and transitions that Gzowski will use during the feature (figure 23). As Gzowski has put it, the purpose of the greens is similar to that of the preparation done for a legal case: "Lawyers are *told* never to ask a question they don't know the answer to; I am *equipped* not to do so" (*The New Morningside Papers* 11).

The greens include actual script but also personal notes from the producer to Gzowski. For a *Morningside* discussion with doctors who do abortions, for example, here is the producer's direct comment, intended to inform Gzowski's progress through the interview: "Peter, I've told them I want *personal* perspectives on how they work the system" (Abley 22).

The producers make sure the guests are available on time, either in person or on the telephone line. They book studios and transportation. They arrange for fees to be paid for certain guests. They read the books that will be featured on the show before Gzowski does. In short, they do everything possible to ensure that Gzowski is thoroughly briefed and prepared and that some six hundred hours of radio every season actually end up on the airwaves.

The producers give yeoman's service on *Morningside*, though most members of Gzowski's radio audience do not think much about who the producers are and what they do. Producers are in the background of media, and in radio the background is dimly lit, indeed. A list of the producers is read after each Friday's broadcast of the *Morningside* season, but Gzowski suggests with

LETTERS # 4---ANTS

SA

PAYMENT TO DOUG HOLMES

FORMAT: TAPE WITH LIVE INTRO AND TAG....

INTRO:

    Today, the last in our series of foreign letters from Doug Holmes. Doug spent four months on an exchange project in southern Borneo. Today he writes about things creepy, crawly.

TAPE:

    IN: "The ants came...

    TIME: 3:05

    OUT: "...BYE FOR NOW. DOUG."

EXTRO:

    Our foreign letters series were written by Doug Holmes while he was on an exchange project in southern Borneo earlier this year.

FIGURE 23

A sample of a "green." Greens include the introductions, notes, questions, and transitions that Peter will use during a Morningside *feature.*

his rapid pace of delivery that this is certainly not the most important part of the week's proceedings. So the producers work hard, try not to complain too much, and remind themselves often that the mention of *Morningside* will look good on their résumés.

SOUNDS OF INTIMACY

The *intimacy* of *Morningside* — and of radio — is created by the immediacy of the human voice and by the high definition of the voice's electronic reproduction. Radio is generally listened to at close quarters. By its isolation of the human voice, radio heightens the illusion that someone is right beside you, speaking in your ear, even speaking from somewhere inside your ear. Marshall McLuhan refers to the voice on radio as a "writer-speaker":

> Radio affects most people intimately, person-to-person, offering a world of unspoken communication between writer-speaker and the listener. That is the immediate aspect of radio. A private experience. (261)

The combination of the words *writer* and *speaker* evokes the dual cognitive effect of radio on the listener. While the *writer* is suggested by the script and calculated pace of radio, the *speaker* is manifest in the voice. David Sexton, a British journalist, puts it this way:

> [T]he pleasure of all radio comes from the unique blend it offers of intimacy and formality, proximity and distance. On the one hand, a voice is physical. You have the speaker breathing with you in the room. The timbre, rhythm, pitch and accent of a voice is distinctive because it is produced from a particular body. In a curious way, you become familiar with that person's actual presence in your home. In another way, of course, one often has no idea of what the person looks like. . . . (11)

The timbre of a particular broadcaster's voice may intensify the illusion of intimacy. Gzowski's voice is musical, strong, percussive, expressive. When combined with the solitary setting in which most radio listeners find themselves (in the car, doing the ironing, driving a tractor), Gzowski's voice is a natural seducer. It is also variable. That helps make every interview different. Depending on the guest, the pitch of his voice oscillates and the pace of his speech is adjusted frequently. His staccato *mm-hm* is used, for example, to urge the interview subject to move on to another point.

Sometimes he stammers; sometimes he doesn't. The stammering is a device. The first purpose of the stammering is to regulate the psychologically controlling nature of his deep voice. Gzowski's voice possesses authority. The stammering helps to foil that authority somewhat, suggesting tentativeness and accessibility. The second purpose is to emphasize the gravity of a topic. It is thus a method for creating a mood.

The third purpose is more specific and is used for prefacing certain questions. It is to convey the impression that he doesn't know anything. This puts a guest off balance, especially if he or she is an expert, allowing Gzowski to bring up controversial questions, or questions dealing with complex issues. As he stammers, he conveys the image of someone reaching for something that only his guests can help him find. This is an appealing attribute in a media interviewer, and I believe that it explains much of Gzowski's popularity. Still, writing of his interviewing style, Gzowski points out that there is also the strategic factor to be considered in this regard: "I . . . tend to move around people's edges until I can see an opening, and then pounce, both off the air and on" (*This Country* 16). Sometimes the volume of his voice is loud, even uproarious; sometimes it is like a whisper. Once, on the sensitive topic of the sexual abuse of children, when he asked his guest, a civil servant, how many men were charged with sexual abuse without being convicted, the question was delivered almost inaudibly. The hushed volume expressed the political explosiveness of the question, but it also conveyed the urgency that the question be answered. Often, his voice is absent. And this is what sets his voice apart from other voices on radio. While the other voices are continually filling in dead air space, Gzowski's is occasionally kept in abeyance, allowing the silence to sing.

These vocal techniques are simply one means of making each interview different. If you listen to other media interviewers, you hear frequent resort to formula. Gzowski's interviews, on the other hand, are organic. They are liquid. He changes the pitch setting, stammering index, volume level, and silence quotient according to the guest and the topic being discussed. He has carried an interview on the history of *Vogue* magazine as compellingly and entertainingly as he has on the Yonge Street riots of 1992, in part because he makes each interview take on a mood and character of its own.

Only on radio can an electronic interviewer make each interview different. On television the stammering or the changes in pitch or volume would either be unnoticeable (in the case of the changes in pitch and volume, since they would be evened out through technology) or cause for the psychological irritation of the audience. A conversation must be frantic on television. Television is shtick; radio aspires to dialogue.

Dialogue is possible for Gzowski because his mode of delivery is not an ironic one. In contrast to many of his colleagues on television and radio (even those on CBC Radio), Gzowski does not have his tongue in his cheek when he intones the introduction to his show. As Doug Whiteway has pointed out, the ironic delivery that characterizes even Gzowski's stand-ins, such as Ian Brown and Ralph Benmergui, is a mask:

[T]he ironist is not bound by what he says. But for those listening there is a consequence. You begin to find such "personalities" curiously detached, and ultimately wearisome: radio versions of the tedious David Letterman who has made media irony, once potent and agile, masscult and moribund. The charm of such people is perishable. But, hey,

in the meantime, they're hip. Life's just a gig. They're cool.
("Cross Current")

When some commentators suggest that Gzowski's voice is deadpan before and after the interviews, this is what they are getting at: Gzowski works continuously to ensure that the medium has the function of refining, focusing, and strengthening the presentation of his personality on radio. This presentation may be many things — the projection of the personal, the fulfilment of ambition, emotional recompensation for private need — but it is not a game or a distraction. When an interview begins, the listener is assured that while some edges of the interviewer's personality have been smoothed, the interviews represent authentic human interaction. Either that — or, as Whiteway puts it, "it's a damn good act. But it's one I'll take."

Gzowski seems unwilling to deny the possibility that his presentation of personality is an "act." He has responded to this sentiment when he has spoken about his approach to interviewing:

I learned early that if you're not interested in a subject, you should fake it. And it's extraordinary how if you fake interest, it actually gets interesting. Someone will start to explain something to you that you didn't think you were interested in, and all of a sudden you think, "This is interesting. I didn't know all that." But sometimes that doesn't work, either. Sometimes it ain't there, and you just want to say, "Who cares?" (Family)

In 1993, the deadpan delivery of introductions and conclusions began to give way more often to improvisation during the program than had occurred in previous seasons. His promotion of the "Best of" version of the program, to be aired that evening, has on more than one occasion taken on the nature of a musing on how the show had gone that day. The perfunctory style that he had used previously to move through this and other duties during the show is not often evident.

Ironically, Gzowski's verbal presentation off the air is different than the one he uses on the radio. In person his voice creates a feeling of greater distance. Talking to Gzowski in his office is not the close-in experience many of his listeners might imagine. He is different in person than he is on radio, and this is to be expected. However, many of his listeners would be surprised at the degree of differences. None of the styles he adopts — none of the voices he uses — is parallel with his "natural" voice and tone.

In person, the resonance of his voice is less characterized by the round, warm tone that listeners recognize on the radio. His voice is consistently sweeter and lower on radio. The fact that he can change the resonance of his voice is not unusual for a performer. Expert singers, for example, become skilled at using the tongue and soft palate to adjust the resonance and tone of their voice. In fact, many singers seek just the kind of resonance Gzowski has on radio. His voice is more relaxed in person; on radio, he is using his voice, consciously or not, to achieve an effect. Gzowski's voice on radio is soothing, in the manner that a rendition of a lullaby by a trained singer might be. In both cases, much effort has gone into preparation, but for the listener that preparation is in the background. Radio technicians can equalize the tone of a voice to make it more resonant, and they are able to reduce excessive hissing in anyone's voice. But in Gzowski's case the tweaking is a process of refining the focus that he has already established.

Another difference, his diction, is a subtler matter. On radio, Gzowski's pronunciation of certain words loses the gentle affectations of class and culture. His enunciation of *s* (as in *yes*), for example, is whispier in person than it is on air. In person, he pronounces the letter *o*, for another example, much more in keeping with his southern Ontario heritage than he does on air; here, the *o* (as in *radio*) sounds something like *ay-oh*. He adds an *oo* sound at the end, something he never does on air. I associate this pronunciation with not only southern Ontario but also portions of the western and mid-western United States. On air, however, the word ends with an abrupt *oh*. Gzowski's radio diction thus serves as a touch of the Canadian vernacular, a symbolic act of inclusion of Atlantic and Western Canadians. If the show is broadcast from Toronto, its host tries to avoid continually implying that fact by his pronunciations.

The verbal presentation is not the only way in which Gzowski differs in person from his radio persona. Face to face, he uses profanity much more often than his radio audience would expect, and he can affect an aggressive stance in daily interactions. Alex Frame, referring to the negotiations that the two have carried on, has said,

> With Peter, if you're straightforward or try to be straightforward, then something appropriate's going to come out of it. If he scares you or intimidates you, then you may as well pack it in and leave the room, because you're dead meat. (*Family*)

GOING WITH THE FLOW

Gzowski has a fatherly voice. It is a deep, controlling voice. To the question, then, of how he has become so successful on a "hot" medium, while adopting a "cool" approach to interviewing, the answer is that the message of the show is one of consolation and comfort. When his listeners are feeling the social rupture that has occurred, for example, in the case of the Oka confrontation of 1990 or the Yonge Street riots of 1992, Gzowski is there to encourage calm by the warm control of his voice. Many Canadians can also imagine his appearance, and that, too, can function as a source of calm (figure 18).

Before and after a disturbing item on his show about racism or violence, the warm voice moves us on to the next item. It is almost impossible without the aid of a tape recorder to determine just what he has said on air. The aural impression created by radio is that every utterance overlaps with another. The voice is one of the means, along with the pacing of the presentation, by which the *flow* of radio is maintained. Without a strong voice, that flow would be interrupted.

The volume and pace of production and distribution of mass media products make it difficult to assess the significance or nature of the messages being conveyed. Studies of mass media and of its significant figures have been hampered by this fact. Like television, radio has established a code for its listeners that specifies how long one person should talk before being interrupted by someone or something else. Radio is suited to the management of contradictions, and Gzowski is an expert practitioner of the medium. He exploits these contradictions in the interests of presenting a popular program.

The tension between the fragmentation of radio's content on the one hand and, on the other, the unifying rhythm of the pacing of the content's presentation can be adjusted endlessly. In doing so, Gzowski unfortunately sometimes makes remarks which, if they were considered seriously, would not stand up to critical scrutiny. For a member of an audience, the flow of radio cannot be stopped, unless a tape recorder is used, which is what I did as I listened to Gzowski's voice on radio and then listened again. That is, I used a technology that would allow me to do what readers, but not radio listeners, can easily do: review, contemplate, conclude, speculate. This allowed me to analyse an example of the importance of flow on *Morningside*.

In April 1992, Gzowski was interviewing Lennox Farrell and his wife, Joan. It was a few days after the Toronto riots, and the Farrells were being interviewed because they are active in the Black Action Defence Committee. As the interview was coming to an end, Gzowski made a statement that was, for those listeners who had the opportunity to reflect on it, the expression of a maudlin sentiment. Gzowski said he hoped that, after retirement, his replacement as host of *Morningside* would be a black woman. He didn't say it in those words, of course. What he did was to set up a question in a way that *implied* he hoped he would be replaced by a black woman. He described a scenario in which the Farrells' granddaughter would be the host of the show. Then he asked them if they thought Canadian society would ever develop to the point that, in this hypothetical situation, no one would notice she was black, that no one would assume she was a "token." Gzowski said,

> Will there be a day — not in my lifetime, probably not in yours, but maybe in my kids' or maybe in your kids' or maybe in my grandchildren's — when the idea of race will have been dropped from this country? So that we won't even notice that the lieutenant-governor is a black man. When your granddaughter is interviewing my granddaughter about her book (and your granddaughter is the host of *Morningside*), no one will say, "And by the way, that's the third host of *Morningside* of African descent." (*Morningside*, April 29, 1992)

The reality at the CBC as elsewhere is that only certain segments of society are represented in positions of power or prestige. The sentiment that it ought to be otherwise is, when expressed by someone of Gzowski's elevated status, charged with ambiguity, regardless of the fact that he is undoubtedly sincere about the matter. Yet to have simply said, "I hope I am replaced by a black woman" would have invited accusations of hypocrisy. To repeat, radio is a flow. Immediately after making this statement, Gzowski was able to move on to another item. A radio audience cannot readily engage in the intellectual reflection needed to translate at all times exactly what is being said.

MORNINGSIDE'S SOCIAL CLEAVAGES

If we assume, as Marshall McLuhan did, that radio is a tribalizing influence, we can observe two tribalizations on *Morningside*, both based on social *cleavages*. The first is that of class. The show is heard in its entirety only on weekday mornings. Many people who work are not able to listen to the show, unless they tune in to the abbreviated "Best of" version, originally at 10:00 p.m., but during 1993–94 at 8:00. While many people at home generally listen while they are doing something else, there is still a measure of leisure associated with the show. Also, the notion of a listener in a car generally assumes, of course, the ownership of a car. This is not to say that only the well-to-do can listen to the show. For his part, Mel Hurtig — wealthy, influential — admits that, as was the case with *This Country in the Morning*, he finds it difficult to listen to *Morningside* because of the time of broadcast.

The other cleavage has to do with the special relationship women have with the show and with Gzowski. Nicole Bélanger, Gzowski's first executive producer at *Morningside*, has said the following about him:

> [He] has sensibilities as a journalist that I used to think were peculiar to women. . . . [Women] tend to see things in a surround, in a context (historical and otherwise) which may come from trying to understand their own evolution. And in an emotional surround women tend to have a better eye. (Crean 132)

The relationship Gzowski has with the women in his audience goes beyond his ability to convey the emotional context for events. In an age when the home has become much more "privatized" than it was previously, say even twenty years ago, radio "delivers" the world to the home. It is a link between the domestic and the public. For women at home, it provides a sense that they are not only being informed about the world, but that they are engaging in some kind of interaction with it.

The typical interaction of this kind is the Camp, Kierans, and Lewis interchange that was held every Tuesday until the 1993–94 season. Here, a civilized chat occurred between three civilized fellows. The sense was that anyone listening was part of the discussion; after all, didn't the three represent the three federal political parties? Yet the information to be found on *Morningside* has been processed and produced. It is not just anyone who called in to talk to Gzowski on Tuesday morning. Similarly, while anyone may write letters to the show, and many listeners do, those letters are processed differentially. A few are read on air, some find their way into one of the *Morningside* books, after editing, and some invite a personal response from Gzowski himself. *Morningside* takes public issues and domesticates them for its audience. For the middle class, and for people bound to the home in particular, this is an important function.

The proposition that listeners consistently form a broad spectrum of Canadian society, then, is unlikely. Instead, a core audience of women at home, even if many of them are there only temporarily or occasionally, is supplemented by a large number of people who listen briefly and sporadically. Many other people listen to the show, of course, but it is the domestication of political and social issues that is *Morningside*'s main function, and women still form the majority of those Canadians who are at home most of the time.

In spite of this, Gzowski says he is conscious as he speaks on radio of an audience that includes more people than the limited segment of Canadian society described here. His professed technique for reaching the number of listeners that he does is to think about people other than the wealthy and powerful:

> I think of ordinary Canadians. There's a lot of truck drivers who listen to hurtin' music on the radio, sure, but there's also a lot of them who listen to us. ("Gzowski's Ordinary People")

"Us" being him.

COMPANIONS FOR THE SOLITARY SOUL

Gzowski has written in his memoirs that when he was beginning his working life, the "newspaper business" appealed to him because of its twin associations of romantic adventure and literary exploit:

I'd written a bit as a student, mostly bad poems and clumsy short stories. I read voraciously, if not well, and many of the people whose work I enjoyed — Hemingway, Lardner, Runyon — had come from newspaper backgrounds. (*The Private Voice* 64)

When he became a *Maclean's* contributor, he would likewise give homage to literary mentors, in this case the members of the Algonquin Round Table, which included such magazine writers as E.B. White and Dorothy Parker:

Almost anything North Americans do, from playing centre field to making mobiles, is done best somewhere in New York. What I do was done best by a group of geniuses who used to meet in the Algonquin Hotel. ("Holiday Weekend" 34)

So Gzowski has fashioned a connection between literary pursuits and journalistic ones at least three times. The first was when he took up newspaper writing. The second was on the occasion of his transition from newspaper writing to magazine writing. And the third took place when his radio programs (beginning with *This Country in the Morning* but most tenaciously with *Morningside*) were first "translated" into book form. The written word forms an anchor for Gzowski's career, from which he departs and returns with varying degrees of commitment.

Morningside's complementary modes are broadcast and book. Radio and the central motif of the *Morningside* books (the letter) are both intimate media. Each is a companion for the solitary soul. The *Morningside* books, like the radio show, are characterized by variety. They can include stories, poems, or interview transcriptions. Also like the radio show, the books have a centrepiece. While the radio show is about Gzowski's interviews, the books are about the audience's letters. Members of the audience write the book, then the book's editor shapes it and offers it back to them. The books are the written expression of the audience's response to Gzowski. Some of the contributors (Myrna Kostash, Timothy Findley, and Sandra Birdsell, for example) are professional writers; others are not. A handful of the contributions are commissioned; most of them are unsolicited letters from listeners. Not surprisingly, most of the submissions are from women. Writing in *The New Morningside Papers*, Gzowski expresses affection for the listeners who write and seems grateful for their contributions: "[N]early all the people whose work appears here are amateurs in the true sense: they write for the love of it" (14). The *Morningside* books are celebrations of Canada's small towns, of simple joys, of Canada's landscape and skyline. Reviewers of the *Morningside* books make a point of observing the compelling nature of the contributions from small-town Canada. The selections represent every corner of rural Canada. Gzowski and the *Morningside* staff presume that listeners in the villages and towns of Canada form an important part of the nation's social and cultural fabric. Each of the pieces in one of the chapters of the second volume of the papers (*The New Morningside Papers*) is devoted to a discussion of why the writer lives in the part of the country he or she does. Most of the writers in the section are talking about small-town or rural Canada. (One of the notable exceptions is Gzowski himself, who explains that he lives in Toronto because he has to.) Indirectly, then, Gzowski's upbringing in Galt finds expression in these books. And of course, for Canadians, the establishment of communication links across the unimaginable distances — by letter and by radio signal — is elemental, a symbol of nationalism, confirmed by Mel Hurtig's comparison of the Canadian Pacific Railway (another nationalist symbol) with *This Country* and *Morningside*.

In the *Morningside* books, the contrast between Gzowski's "voice" as a writer and his "voice" as a radio host becomes sharper. It is in the introductions and interludes in these books that he reveals the touches of his former life as a journalist. The writer is eloquent, loquacious, even long-winded; the host of *Morningside* is reticent, stammering, preferring simple declarative sentences. The writer drops names mercilessly, revealing his personal and professional ties to Canada's élite. The radio host doesn't generally let on during an interview that he knows his famous guest personally. The writer is much more likely than the radio personality to venture a firm opinion on, say, a political matter. The writer is literary, clear, articulate, while the host is folksy, charmingly clumsy. The writer, in short, is an extrovert and the host an introvert.

Some listeners express indignation at the fact that Gzowski seems content to have other people write books that become best sellers to his authorial and financial credit. (The contributors to the book sign a copyright release in exchange for a copy of the book upon publication.) He writes an introduction to each book and provides commentary throughout and an essay or two, so his role is really that of collector, although he is cited as author.

The argument against this is, of course, that the *Morningside* books would not exist without Gzowski's influence and personality. The show was not the same when it was hosted by Gzowski's predecessor, Don Harron, and it will not be the same after he leaves. Gzowski invokes a distinctive, amiable, letter-writing response from his audience. The "wave of empathy" he sets in motion across the country is his alone, and for that he deserves the title of author of these books. I hope there are several more to come.

THE PRIVATE VOICE

The Private Voice was published in 1988. Gzowski's ninth book, it is subtitled "A Journal of Reflections." However, the book offers few insights into Gzowski's intimate thoughts and musings, except those connected to the limited number of biographical facts he has revealed elsewhere. There is a sense of reserve in the book, although its prose is invariably endearing. The book exemplifies Gzowski as the private figure masquerading as a public figure. In John Bemrose's words (in the *Maclean's* magazine review of the book), *The Private Voice* is a "hybrid of memoir and subjective reportage":

> Writing about his youth is disappointingly brief and guarded. . . . For most memoirists, the first 20 years of life are the source of their richest insights. But for Gzowski, that period is clearly a minefield to be avoided. (67)

Asked what he'll do if he did in fact leave out a discussion of important aspects of his personal life as he wrote the book, he drily states, "I'll probably get up from my grave and do another draft on my tombstone" (Miller 28). Like *Spring Tonic*, *The Private Voice* was written at a time of transition for Gzowski. In 1987, he had felt as if it might be time to leave *Morningside*. While he and I spoke in the spring of that year, the drawer of the desk on which my tape recorder rested held his contract for services for the following season, unsigned. That year, he waited until the last possible moment to complete the transaction. The book was a form of self-study Gzowski had initiated to try to plumb his own feelings about his life and work.

That this process of reflection should also have the function of resulting in a book is, as with *Spring Tonic*, significant. *Spring Tonic* provided a sort of emotional wake-up call for Gzowski. He took spiritual strength from compiling it, though its poor sales discouraged him. In addition to serving to resolve the contradictions of the aural and the visual, then, the publication of a book takes the function of a personal marker for Gzowski. It temporarily slows or stops the flow of radio.

THE HONOURS

Gzowski's *Morningside* years have been blessed by a measure of public recognition that is rarely accorded a member of the media. Occasionally, Gzowski expresses his bewilderment at the notion of a radio broadcaster receiving recognition of this kind, but he enjoys and accepts the honours with grace:

These have been rich and satisfying years for me. . . . [They] have given me a ringside seat — sometimes indeed I feel as if it were a seat inside the ring — for all the great social and political changes that have swept Canada. It is a lovely job. ("Convocation")

He has received several honorary degrees, and in 1986 was named an Officer of the Order of Canada. The citations for these honours generally refer to Gzowski's contribution to some aspect of the "Canadian identity." The honours are connected to his articulation of nationalism. The *Morningside* program and books appeal to a patriotic sense in many Canadians, and the honours Gzowski receives are testimony to this fact.

The charity to which Gzowski has consistently lent his name and dedication is adult literacy. His golf tournaments for literacy ("Peter Gzowski's Invitationals") take place across the country — a dozen or so annually. Celebrities golf, and money is raised for funding programs to encourage adults to learn to read. The tournaments are carried out in association with Frontier College, an adult education institution in Ontario.

The Invitationals are effective in raising money. A single tournament held in Calgary in 1990, for example, raised a little more than $78,000. The direct expenses, which include such things as a buffet lunch for the players, came to about $6,000. The Learning Centre Adult Literacy Program in Calgary received more than $72,000, which was used in order to train and coordinate volunteer literacy tutors, improve its library collection, and hold workshops on literacy throughout Alberta. The money comes mainly from celebrities and others who pay a couple of hundred dollars to golf with Gzowski. Other fund-raising techniques associated with the Invitationals include auctioning the caddying services or donated possessions of famous Canadians. In Yukon in 1992, for example, someone paid $2,100 for the privilege of having Cynthia Dale, of *Street Legal* fame, hand the clubs over as required; someone else paid a similar amount to have Audrey McLaughlin, the national leader of the New Democratic Party, do the same thing. Later, someone bid $650 for Ms Dale's *Street Legal* jacket. All of this is documented in a kind of annual report published by the organizers of the Invitationals, entitled, quaintly, *Reading the Greens*, which evokes at once, of course, Gzowski's three occupations: golf, radio (the producer's "greens," as well as the golfer's links), and the written word. A distinguishing feature of the Invitationals is the naming of a poet laureate. Dennis Lee, Margaret Atwood, and Bronwen Wallace, among others, have done the honours. The poet spends the day with the golfers and is invited to address the gathering in the evening with an original poem. The poets' addresses lend a spiritual tone to the proceedings, as Gzowski points out: "These have been stirring moments for me, a reminder of the role poetry must have played in society before even the days of radio" ("Convocation").

Gzowski works hard at organizing and carrying out the tournaments. We can think of his claim that he is a "writer who's now working in radio" and the implicit importance he attaches, as a romantic traditionalist, to the written word. Also, as Gzowski says, and as Hurtig's experience confirms, the *Morningside* audience is a literate one. If he is a surrogate listener, then he may encourage, on behalf of his audience, the goal of literacy for all. Here is how chapter four of *The Fourth Morningside Papers* begins:

> *Morningside*'s listeners must be, as I've said elsewhere, the most literate radio audience in the world, and in the seasons this book encompasses, they continued their watch over our use (and sometimes misuse) of language. (108)

It is symbolically fitting that Gzowski has donated his energy and reputation to a charity that is devoted to the written word. Beginning with the British annuals of his childhood, Gzowski has found in reading and writing a means by which a personal and cultural identity can be fashioned. As a newspaper carrier, he delivered the written word to his neighbours daily. As a

FIGURE 24

Morningside *(1994)*.
PHOTO COURTESY THE CBC

"writer-speaker," he repeats the task today. The "writer who's now working in radio" publicly supports the effort to encourage literacy.

5. *The Galt* Daily Reporter

The downy snows in Galt — we'll put out of mind the unfriendly change of the city's name — are cliffs on either side of the path of Peter Gzowski, aged fourteen. They have been shovelled by the good residents of the town, whose newspapers Peter now tows. He has a wagon — no, a toboggan — to aid his progress.

The Canadian newspaper carrier is an entrepreneur. He or she takes a risk, accepting the product on spec. The papers are not consigned to the aspiring youngster, but sold wholesale. The profit to be made is in correlation to the accuracy of the estimated sales. The lessons of thrift and efficiency, as well as the habit of ambition, are learned quickly in such an endeavour. Decades later, Peter's fealty to the preparations required for an installment of *Morningside* would extend to setting his alarm clock to 4:44 a.m. and then to 4:14 a.m. as the flow of mail to the show strengthened. Such diligence may well have been instilled by the rigours of his duties as a newspaper carrier; the particular practice was not, since the *Reporter* was an afternoon paper.

Let us compare once more the paper that Peter delivered — and, for that matter, all the others like it in Canada, but especially those in southern Ontario, since most other parts of the country did not have the weight of establishment to give rise to such a medium — to the radio show for which he would become best known. I have suggested that the *Reporter* provided news in a style that was at once eclectic and entertaining. *Morningside*, too, is current, informative, by turns sobering and hilarious, professionally paced, and carefully written and produced. As with the *Reporter*, the values it espouses are not articulated directly; instead, they form part of a total experience for the listener. The world, particularly Canadian society, is presented not as a complex phenomenon with which the intellect must contend but a *ground* for the *figure* of media.

Did young Peter take some professional pride in his job? He must have. The papers would have been folded smartly and left nestled in their boxes. If a home had no box, Peter would have set the paper safely behind the screen door. Especially if the home, say one on exclusive Blair Road, just a street over from his own on Park Avenue, belonged to the Chaplins or some other family whose name would eventually appear in the social web to be drawn from *An Unbroken Line*.

With the evidence we now have in hand of the depth of Peter's later interest in matters journalistic, we may assume that in his daily rounds he would have glanced at the headlines, perhaps stopped to read a story or two. Since he delivered papers just after World War II, he would have read stories about the defence of the Empire. In that case, he would have felt a twinge of pride that Sir Casimir, his ancestor, had in his old age been named an aide-de-camp to Queen Victoria. He would also have felt a sense of satisfaction that the news — duly observed and recorded, prepared for publication, and printed — was in his hands, about to reach its audience. The story was on its last leg of the journey. And as he would continue to do some forty years later, he fulfilled his duty. He gently nudged the story to its destination.

A CONCLUSION

At Dundas and Bathurst, near Chinatown in Toronto, is a green spot called Alexandra Park. The park has a skating arena, pool, ball diamond, tennis court, playground, and library. In the morning, old men and women limber up in groups of a dozen, doing slow calisthenics or *tai chi*. This is where Sir Casimir used to keep his garden. He is said to have been a lover of flowers. His residence, called "The Hall," was a centre of refined social activity in Toronto. It was to be seized from his descendants by the city for unpaid property taxes.

I have referred to the personal mythology that has informed the events of Peter Gzowski's life and career. The most resilient motive of that mythology is the small town, with its related associations of Sir Casimir's contributions to Canadian society. The small town influenced both Peter's childhood and his later stance as a radio interviewer. What does one do when the vision, the personal mythology that one has fashioned, does not mesh with one's perceptions? What happens when the ideal with which one illuminated the beginnings of an undertaking becomes swamped by connections, electricity, funk? When it becomes evident that Canada is not a small town but, like other social experiments, simply a cacophony of questions — cultural noise — whose answers give voice to yet more questions?

For Gzowski, the stammering index could rise, and this might well give good returns. A suggestion of panic, it may invite others to take the floor and speak. It could put at risk the act of closure that some would favour. It might cause those of us at this end of the electrical current's flow, those inhabiting as audience the resonant space of radio, to turn to others in seeking something that only they can help us find.

Giraffe-like in bodily carriage, vaguely graceful, a sexagenarian Peter has etherized. He has gone electric. The aspirations he held early have enacted this transformation. When ill as a child, he would lie abed, listening to the hum and hiss of the radio, finding comfort in the promise of identity. When Peter entered adolescence, the written word became source-code for heritage. The word would be *spoken* when, as an adult, he took his place behind the microphone. Radio would become a refuge for the "writer-speaker." From that private survey Gzowski could speak to a nation. The nation, in turn, could laud the achievement of an individual, an accomplishment that as corporate body would be denied. The country would dream him into existence, while the rails of the first national dream were being lifted. The dissonance among the three lives of the broadcaster would be subsumed in the dreaming. The dream of an electric life would be expressed by community, connections, and dialogue, which are the informing principles of the life lived.

Thus we may speculate on the secret nature of Peter Gzowski's appeal as a broadcaster. He has activated some corporate adrenaline in an audience, and it has given energy to him. His true function is not to deal with or assuage disparate claims but to give them succour. Given a voice, these articulations lose their violence. It is not a town-hall meeting, "a village bulletin board for the nation," over which Gzowski presides, as he would have it, but a northern wailing wall.

Our conversation is ending. I ask Peter Gzowski what he hopes his children will say about him. What will the romantic traditionalist actually *say* when it comes time to pass on his most closely held convictions about heritage? He pauses. "Oh, dear. . . . That I wasn't embarrassed to be wrong," he says tentatively and changes the subject so that he can talk about his parents for a while. Then, as he pauses to smile, an epiphany:

> I want my children to know that there are other things on my mind than coming in to the radio station every day and asking people questions. ("Interview," 1987 [Adria])

CHRONOLOGY

1934   Peter John Gzowski is born on Friday, July 13, in
        Toronto, to Harold and Margaret Gzowski.
1938   After separating from Peter's father, Margaret marries
        Reg Brown. The family takes up residence in Galt (now
        Cambridge), Ontario.
1948   Peter delivers the Galt *Daily Reporter* and the London
        Free Press in his neighbourhood.
1949   Attends Ridley College, St. Catharines, Ontario, until
        1952, on the advice of his father and paternal grand-
        father. Gzowski's great-great-grandfather, Sir Casimir
        Gzowski, who was a Polish émigré, first visited St.
        Catharines in the 1830s while seeking business for the
        Pennsylvania firm for which he worked. He would
        settle in Canada in 1841.
1950   Margaret Young Brown, Gzowski's mother, dies.
1952   Gzowski attends classes at the University of Toronto.
1954   With the assistance of a family friend, Gzowski takes
        the job of advertising salesman, then reporter based in
        Kapuskasing, at the Timmins *Daily Press*.
1955   Attends University of Toronto, until 1957, but leaves
        the institution without completing a degree. He also
        fulfils his duties as a police reporter for the Toronto
        Telegram while continuing to attend classes at university.
1956   While attending the University of Toronto, Gzowski
        takes a job at the university's student newspaper, *The
        Varsity*, as editor, an elected position, until 1957.
1957   After taking a train west, Gzowski becomes a reporter
        at the Moose Jaw *Times-Herald*.
1958   Marries Jenny Lissaman in February. The couple takes

up residence in Chatham, Ontario. Gzowski becomes managing editor of the Chatham *Daily News*, then assistant editor at *Maclean's*, replacing Christina McCall. The first of his five children, Peter Casimir, is born.

1960   Appointed Preview editor, *Maclean's*.

1961   Appointed Quebec editor, *Maclean's*.

1962   Appointed managing editor, *Maclean's*.

1963   The University of Western Ontario awards Gzowski its President's Medal for excellence in magazine writing.

1964   Effective the issue of September 19, Gzowski resigns from *Maclean's*.

1965   "Song for Canada," co-written by "Pete" Gzowski and Ian Tyson, is released on Ian and Sylvia's album *Early Morning Rain*.

1965   With sport writer Trent Frayne, Gzowski publishes *Great Canadian Sports Stories: A Century of Competition*, a collection of essays on Canadian heroes of sport.

1967   Takes the job of editor at the *Star Weekly*.

1968   The *Star Weekly* goes out of business. With his wife and children, Gzowski sails to England on the *Aleksandr Pushkin*.

1969   Takes the job of host of *Radio Free Friday* on CBC Radio. That year, he also fills in for the regular host of *Gerussi*. Returning to *Maclean's* in late autumn, Gzowski becomes the editor, leaving the magazine during the summer of 1970.

1971   His first extended project on radio, *This Country in the Morning*, is hosted by Gzowski until 1974.

1974   After encouragement from Mel Hurtig, the Edmonton publisher, *Peter Gzowski's Book About This Country in the Morning* is published. The book becomes the number-one best seller in Canada, selling some 44,000 copies. Gzowski ends *This Country in the Morning* but hosts a CBC Stereo show entitled *Gzowski on FM* until 1976. Gzowski receives an ACTRA award for broadcasting.

1976   With Alex Frame, his producer from *This Country*,

Gzowski helps create *90 Minutes Live* for CBC Television, with Gzowski as host. The show, modelled on American programs such as *The Tonight Show*, is cancelled after Gzowski resigns in 1978.

1977 Gzowski separates from his wife.

1978 Harold Gzowski, Peter's natural father, dies. Peter moves to Rockwood, Ontario, to reconsider his career and personal life.

1979 Hoping to publish a book as successful as *Peter Gzowski's Book About This Country in the Morning*, Gzowski publishes *Spring Tonic*, a book about spring. The book does not do as well as Gzowski's first book, selling only a couple of thousand copies, and his professional relationship with Hurtig ends.

1980 Publishes *The Sacrament*, a book about the ordeal of two Canadian survivors of an airplane crash. The book reveals the techniques and aspirations of the New Journalism.

1981 *The Game of Our Lives* is published, a tribute to hockey and to the Edmonton Oilers. Gzowski is appointed host of *Morningside*, CBC Radio, replacing Don Harron.

1982 Publishes *An Unbroken Line*, the story of thoroughbred racing in Ontario. The focal connection to be made in the book is that Sir Casimir Gzowski established the Queen's Plate in 1860.

1984 Conferred with an honorary Doctor of Letters by the University of New Brunswick on May 24.

1985 *Gzowski & Co.* is broadcast on CBC Television. As with Gzowski's first project on television, the ratings are not as high as expected and the show is cancelled in 1987. Gzowski publishes *The Morningside Papers*, based on his radio show. The book becomes a best seller, as do its sequels.

1986 Named an Officer of the Order of Canada on November 12.

1987 Contemplates leaving *Morningside*, but decides against it. *The New Morningside Papers* appears. He receives an honorary Doctor of Laws from two more Canadian universities: from the University of Windsor on June 15, and from Trent University on October 31.

1988   Publishes *The Private Voice: A Journal of Reflections*, a book of memoirs. He also publishes *A Sense of Tradition*, a book honouring the centennial of Ridley College.

1989   *The Latest Morningside Papers* appears.

1990   Conferred with an honorary Doctor of Laws from Queen's University on June 2.

1991   *The Fourth Morningside Papers* appears.

1992   In September, Gzowski begins his second decade as the host of *Morningside*.

1993   In May, Gzowski is reported taking a smoking break with fellow CBC employees *outside* the corporation's new broadcast centre in Toronto. Gzowski had previously declined to observe the CBC's no-smoking policy.

WORKS CONSULTED

Abley, Mark. "Gzowski Then and Now." *Saturday Night* Nov. 1986: 19–28.

Adria, Marco. "Where Are the Heroes?: An Interview with Murray McLauchlan." *Aurora* Autumn 1988: 38–41.

Bemrose, John. "King of the Airwaves: The Memoirs of a Celebrated Broadcaster." *Maclean's* Nov. 7, 1988: 67.

Bird, Roger, ed. *Documents of Canadian Broadcasting*. Ottawa: Carleton UP, 1988.

Bossin, Bob. Interview on August 20, 1993. Edmonton, Alberta. Marco Adria.

Crean, Susan. *Newsworthy: The Lives of Media Women*. Toronto: Stoddart, 1985.

Eco, Umberto. *Foucault's Pendulum*. Translated from the Italian by William Weaver. New York: Ballantine, 1990.

Edel, Leon. *Writing Lives*. New York: Norton, 1987.

Family: A Loving Look at CBC Radio. National Film Board, 1991. Produced by Adam Symansky. Begun by Donald Brittain and completed by writer/narrator Robert Duncan.

Frayne, Trent, and Peter Gzowski. *Great Canadian Sports Stories: A Century of Competition*. Toronto: Canadian Centennial Library, 1965.

Fulford, Robert. *Best Seat in the House: Memoirs of a Lucky Man*. Toronto: Collins, 1988.

Gzowski, Peter. "What It's Like to Have a Famous (But Forgotten) Ancestor." *Maclean's* May 23, 1959: 24–25, 32–35.

———. "Holiday Weekend in New York." *Maclean's* July 2, 1960: 23–25, 32–35.

———. "The Raffish Tradition of the College Football Weekend." *Maclean's* Dec. 17, 1960: 26–27, 34–36.

———. "My First Negro." *Maclean's* Apr. 22, 1961: 30, 66–69.

———. "The Time the Schick Hit the Fan and Other Adventures at

Maclean's." *The Canadian Forum* Oct. 1964: 150–52.

———. "The Global Village Has Everything But Surprises." *Saturday Night* Dec. 1968: 33–36.

———. "How You Gonna Keep 'em Down on the Farm After They've Said **** You?" *Saturday Night* May 1969: 29–31.

———. *Peter Gzowski's Book About This Country in the Morning.* Edmonton: Hurtig, 1974.

———. *Spring Tonic.* Edmonton: Hurtig, 1979.

———. *The Sacrament: A True Story of Survival.* Toronto: McClelland, 1980.

———. *The Game of Our Lives.* Toronto: McClelland, 1981.

———. *An Unbroken Line.* Toronto: McClelland, 1982.

———. *The Morningside Papers.* Toronto: McClelland, 1985.

———. *The New Morningside Papers.* Toronto: McClelland, 1987.

———. Interview on 28 Apr. 1987. Toronto, Ontario. Marco Adria.

———. *A Sense of Tradition: A Century of Ridley College Memories, 1889–1989.* Sutton: Hedge Road Press, 1988.

———. *The Private Voice: A Journal of Reflections.* Toronto: McClelland, 1988.

———. *The Latest Morningside Papers.* Toronto: McClelland, 1989.

———. Convocation Address at Queen's University on June 2, 1990. Kingston, Ontario.

———. *The Fourth Morningside Papers.* Toronto: McClelland, 1991.

———. Interview on May 26, 1992. Toronto, Ontario. Marco Adria.

———. *Canadian Living.* McClelland, 1993.

Hurtig, Mel. Interview on May 11, 1992. Edmonton, Alberta. Marco Adria.

Kos-Rabcewicz-Zubkowski, Ludwik, and William Edward Greening. *Sir Casimir Stanislaus Gzowski: A Biography.* Toronto: Burns and MacEachern, 1959.

Marchand, Philip. *Marshall McLuhan: The Medium and the Messenger.* Toronto: Random, 1989.

McLuhan, Marshall. *Understanding Media: The Extensions of Man.* New York: New American Library, 1964.

Miller, Donna S. "Gzowski Spills His Guts." *Chatelaine* Oct. 1988: 28.

Powe, B.W. *The Solitary Outlaw.* Toronto: Lester, 1987.

Ramp, Bill. Interview on May 29, 1992. Peterborough, Ontario. Marco Adria.

Remington, Bob. "Gzowski's Ordinary People Far from Ordinary."
Edmonton Journal Nov. 8, 1987: C1.

Sexton, David. "The Faces We Don't Want to See." *Sunday Telegraph*
May 16, 1993: 11.

Whiteway, Doug. "Cross Current." *Globe and Mail* Sept. 16, 1992: A10.

Wilson, Edmund. *O Canada: An American's Notes on Canadian Culture.*
New York: Farrar, 1965.